The Country Houses, Castles and Mansions of Renfrewshire

John Fyfe Anderson

Ardgowan House

In 1403 the lands of Ardgowan were granted to John Stewart, whose father was King Robert III of Scotland, and these have passed by direct line of descent to Sir Ludovic Houston Shaw-Stewart, twelfth Baronet of Greenock and Blackhall, who inherited his title in 2004. The first baronetcy was conferred on Archibald Stewart (1635 – c.1722) by King Charles I. Sir John Stewart, fourth Baronet, inherited the western half of Greenock in 1752 after the death of his great-uncle, Sir John Shaw, third and last Baronet of Greenock. From this time he assumed the extra surname of Shaw as did his descendants. Ardgowan House was built between 1798 and 1801 and is situated in a dominating position on the south shore of the River Clyde near Inverkip. The architect was Hugh Cairncross and the parkland surrounding the house was designed by James Ramsay in 1797. The interior of the house was furnished by Gillow of Lancaster and the walls were hung with paintings which had been collected on various Grand Tours of Europe. There were also family portraits by Sir Henry Raeburn. The Shaw-Stewart family have a long record of distinguished public service from the eighteenth century until recent times. The fifth, seventh, eighth and ninth Baronets held office as Lord Lieutenants of Renfrewshire and the fourth, sixth, seventh and eighth Baronets have served as MPs at Westminster. Ardgowan House is still the home of the Shaw-Stewarts but also hosts corporate entertaining and educational courses and offers exclusive accommodation.

Text © John Fyfe Anderson, 2013.
First published in the United Kingdom, 2013,
by Stenlake Publishing Ltd.
Telephone: 01290 551122
www.stenlake.co.uk

ISBN 9781840336160

**The publishers regret that they cannot supply
copies of any pictures featured in this book**

Acknowledgements

Thanks to the staffs of Reference and Local Studies, Paisley Central Library, and the Watt Library, Greenock, for their assistance.

Auchengrange House

Auchengrange was built about 1832 and was formerly known as Wattieston. It was originally a two-storey Georgian country house but various additions were made later in the nineteenth century. These can be seen on the left of this photograph from around 1910, but were later demolished and the house remodelled. A distinctive feature of this property is the wide porch at the front entrance with its Corinthian columns. The house is situated in attractive grounds with an area of mature woodland, a grassy paddock and a curling pond, and is located one and a half miles east of Lochwinnoch at Auchengrange Hill. There are fine views from the house looking towards Castle Semple Loch and over to the hills of Muirshiel Country Park. Auchengrange was granted B Listed Building status in 1983.

Introduction

The area which later formed the historic county of Renfrewshire belonged to the ancient Caledonian tribe of the Damnonii and became part of the Kingdom of Strathclyde. The western part known as Strathgryffe was granted to Walter Fitzalan (1106 – 1177), the first High Steward of Scotland, by King David I. Before 1404 Renfrewshire was contained within the county of Lanark but became a separate county in that year when King Robert III granted his son and heir James (later King James I of Scotland) the Barony of Renfrew. Since that time the eldest sons of Scottish monarchs (and of British monarchs after the Union of the Crowns in 1603) have held the title of Baron of Renfrew. The Prince of Wales is the 29th Baron of Renfrew.

This volume contains a selection of country houses, mansions and castles in Renfrewshire from the fifteenth to the nineteenth centuries. Some of these properties have been demolished, others remain occupied, and a number of them have been converted into apartments. The owners of these buildings have been many and varied including aristocratic and landed families who have owned their estates for centuries. For example, the Shaw-Stewart family have been associated with the Ardgowan estate in Inverkip since the fifteenth century. Other properties have been built by successful businessmen and traders such as Sir Thomas Glen-Coats of the Paisley thread manufacturers J. and P. Coats. Some owners in past centuries were unable to maintain their properties due to their financial circumstances and as a result the houses became derelict and were later demolished. Other properties were severely damaged by fire and met the same fate.

Renfrewshire presently consists of three unitary council areas known as Renfrewshire, East Renfrewshire and Inverclyde. In former times the county included areas which have been incorporated within the city of Glasgow and a number of mansions and castles in this volume come into this category. Pollok House, Pollok Castle, Langside House, Jordanhill House, Scotstoun House, Thornliebank House, Auldhouse, Crookston Castle and Haggs Castle were formerly located in Renfrewshire.

Many architectural styles are represented in this volume and many well known architects were involved in the design of the various country houses and mansions. These include David Bryce (1803 – 1876) who perfected the Scottish Baronial style. One of his outstanding designs was that of Craigends House. The renowned Adam family are also represented, William Adam (1654 – 1748) having designed Pollok House. His sons, Robert Adam (1728 – 1792) and James Adam (1732 – 1794), were responsible for designing Caldwell House.

These country houses and mansions required large workforces to keep them operating. Butlers, valets, ladies' maids, housemaids, cooks, housekeepers, gardeners, coachmen and later chauffeurs were all part of the daily life of a grand mansion. In the mid 1880s in Renfrewshire 1,141 men and 7,623 women were employed as domestic servants. The largest sector of employment for women in Scotland until the Second World War was domestic service.

A number of houses and estates are open to the public on a regular basis. In some instances the National Trust for Scotland has assumed responsibility for properties such as Pollok House and the gardens of Greenbank House, Clarkston. Many of the mansions still remaining in Renfrewshire are listed buildings, thus ensuring the retention of their original design if restoration takes place. Historic Scotland lists buildings which are considered worthy of preservation and provides grants for repairs.

Renfrewshire did not experience the massive industrial expansion of Glasgow and many of its country houses and mansions remain an important part of Scotland's heritage and are an asset to be retained and preserved. They demonstrate the changing face of architecture over the centuries from defensive structures to those that were solely for residential purposes. It is fortunate that a number of them have been well maintained for the present and future generations.

Balclutha House

Balclutha was located in Newark Street, Greenock, and was built in the 1880s. The mansion was considered to be one of the finest in the west end of the town and its grandeur was emphasised by the great chandelier which hung from the dome of the entrance hall. A prominent owner of this property was Robert Lyons Scott (1871 – 1939) who was Chairman of Scott's Shipbuilding and Engineering Company (later Scott Lithgow) from 1915 until 1939. He was also a big game hunter and went on many expeditions in Africa. His hunting trophies were displayed throughout the mansion and he also possessed an outstanding collection of ancient weapons. In his will he left this collection to the Corporation of the City of Glasgow who made arrangements for its housing in the Kelvingrove Art Gallery and Museum. Glasgow Museums also has a collection of over 3,000 books and manuscripts which belonged to Scott. This collection is one of the three most extensive collections in the world and is concerned with every aspect of military theory and practice. At the beginning of the Second World War in 1939 Balclutha was purchased as accommodation for members of the Women's Royal Naval Service (Wrens). In 1945 the mansion was converted into a hostel for civilian staff who worked in the Torpedo Experimental Establishment at Fort Matilda. This hostel was closed in 1955 and this magnificent property was demolished the following year.

Barochan House

The Barochan estate was in the possession of the Fleming family from the thirteenth century. William Fleming of Barochan is mentioned as witness to a charter granted by Malcolm, Earl of Lennox, to Walter Spruel in the reign of Alexander III who was king of Scotland from 1249 – 1286. One of his descendants, also William Fleming, perished at the Battle of Flodden in 1513 along with six of his sons. The last member of this family associated with Barochan was Jane Fleming who died in 1863. The first home of the family on this estate was located on a hill north of Houston but it was destroyed by fire and was replaced by a castle at the end of the sixteenth century. Extensions were added to the property in the eighteenth century. In 1896 the imposing mansion shown here was built in the Arts and Crafts Baronial style and incorporated the tower of the old castle. Most of Barochan House was demolished in 1947 with only a portion from the late nineteenth century remaining. A notable resident of Barochan House in the late nineteenth and early twentieth century was Sir Charles Bine Renshaw (1848 – 1918) who served as Conservative MP for the Western Division of Renfrewshire from 1892 to 1906. His baronetcy was awarded in 1903. Sir Charles was a former chairman of the Caledonian Railway Company. One of his recreations was gardening and he had a large collection of flowering shrubs in the grounds of the house. The property is situated two miles north-east of Bridge of Weir.

Barshaw House

Barshaw House was built in the early nineteenth century by Robert Smith. It was later purchased by James Arthur who built further extensions and also totally redesigned the interior. One of the main features of this property was the conservatory which can be seen on the left of this view. James Arthur was born in Paisley in 1819 and was involved in business there as a young man. In the 1840s he joined in partnership with Hugh Fraser and established a drapery business at the corner of Buchanan Street and Argyle Street in Glasgow. This business was known as Arthur and Fraser. In 1860 James Arthur founded Arthur and Company which became the largest wholesale drapery business in the United Kingdom. He also had further extensive business interests in shipping, was one of the founders of Young's Paraffin Company, and was involved in business until his death in 1885. Barshaw House is located at the back of Barshaw Park in the east end of Paisley. The grounds, which amounted to 55 acres, were purchased by Paisley Town Council from the Arthur family in 1911 and officially opened as a public park the following year. The mansion was converted into a maternity and child welfare unit nine years later and continued in this purpose until 1959, becoming a geriatric hospital in 1961. It has now been converted into flats.

Blythswood House was designed by James Gillespie Graham and built between 1820 and 1822 for Major Archibald Campbell. It was originally situated in the middle of an extensive plantation where the River Cart joined with the River Clyde. The mansion had a total of 118 rooms and within the grounds there were two curling ponds, a farm, a coal mine, a cricket pitch, two tennis courts, two bowling greens, and nine-hole and nineteen-hole golf courses. A number of gardeners tended apricot, fig, melon and plum trees. Major Archibald Campbell served as an MP for various periods from 1806 to 1831, representing the different constituencies of Glasgow Burghs, Elgin Burghs and Perth Burghs. He died unmarried in 1838. The mansion and estate were inherited by a relative, Archibald Douglas, who changed his name to Campbell. His son, also Archibald Campbell (1837 – 1908), was created a baronet in 1880 and became the first Lord Blythswood in 1892. He had served as a Lieutenant-Colonel of the Scots Guards during the Crimean War and was MP for the Western Division of Renfrewshire in 1873/74 and from 1885 to 1892. Lord Blythswood was also Colonel and A.D.C to Queen Victoria, who resided at Blythswood House in August 1888 on the occasion of her opening the new City Chambers in Glasgow. During the demolition of the mansion in 1935 an underground passage was discovered; it is thought that this may have led at one time to the ancient castle of Renfrew.

Broadstone House

Broadstone House just east of Port Glasgow was built in 1869/70 by David Bryce in the Scottish Baronial style with some of its details based on nearby Newark Castle. The property was constructed for John and Helen Birkmyre whose names were inscribed on a plaque above the front door. John Birkmyre (1834 – 1910), of the Gourock Ropework Company in Port Glasgow, was known for his many public benefactions and his generosity to those in need. Broadstone House was built in greyish-pink sandstone with a four-storey tower and a distinctive stone-framed conservatory. The grounds had a walled garden which was tended by a large team of gardeners. In 1918 the mansion with its estate of 59 acres was purchased by George Anderson Tombazis who was the Greek consul in Glasgow. Eleven years later the property was converted into a psychiatric hospital known as Broadfield. This hospital closed in 1985 and it was sold at auction in 2001 for £725,000 to Muir Homes. It was intended that the former Broadstone House would be the centrepiece of the Castlebank residential development with its conversion into luxury apartments but a fire in 2004 reduced the building to a shell and work was delayed. The conversion has since taken place and luxury villas have been built in the grounds.

Burnbrae House was built about 1830 for the Speirs family on the south bank of the Black Cart. It was Alexander Speirs (1714 – 1782) who had established the family fortune as one of Glasgow's leading tobacco lords and his son, Archibald, inherited his father's business interests. Burnbrae House was one of the finest mansions in Renfrewshire with its turreted roof, stone-carved balustrades, pillared porches and bay windows. It was surrounded by woodland and a former head gardener at Burnbrae House was John Gilmartin after whom Gilmerton Road in Linwood was named. Burnbrae was demolished in 1940 and the site was later occupied by the car park of a car factory. This was Rootes Motors, which began car production in Linwood in 1963. The plant was taken over in 1967 by the Chrysler Corporation and a further change of ownership occurred in 1979 when Peugeot-Citroen took over car production and renamed the company Talbot. However, in 1981 all car production ceased at Linwood resulting in unemployment for thousands of workers. One member of the Speirs family was Lady Anne Speirs whose father was Jacob Pleydell-Bouverie, fourth Earl of Radnor. In 1867 she married Archibald Alexander Speirs, Laird of Houston. Lady Anne was responsible for promoting the art of embroidery as a village industry in nearby Houston.

Caldwell House

Caldwell House was erected in the south-east corner of the parish of Neilston, close to the boundary between Renfrewshire and Ayrshire. The earliest known owners of the estate were the Caldwells, one of whom was Chancellor of Scotland in 1349. This mansion was designed by the brothers James and Robert Adam and completed in 1773. It was the third home of the Caldwells to be built on the estate, the first being the old castle of Caldwell, which was the principal residence of the family from the fourteenth century. It was located on a knoll to the south-west of Lochlibo. A new house was built in 1712 by William Mure on the lands of Ramshead. Caldwell House was built under the instructions of his son, William Mure, Baron of the Scottish Exchequer. This mansion remained the family home of the Mures until 1909. In 1927 the Govan District Health Board acquired the property and converted it into a hospital for mentally handicapped children. This closed in 1985. In 1987 the estate was sold off in lots by the government. The house was seriously damaged by fire in 1995 and the roof was destroyed, thus reducing this once magnificent building to a state of dereliction.

Capelrig House

The lands of Capelrig belonged to the Knights Templar in the twelfth century and later to the Knights Hospitallers who had their headquarters at Torphichen. The lands of the Knights Hospitallers were given over to the Crown at the time of the Scottish Reformation in 1560. However, Mary, Queen of Scots, restored them to Sir James Sandilands (c.1511 – 1579), first Lord Torphichen and last Preceptor of the Knights Hospitallers in Scotland. The lands of Capelrig thus came into the possession of Lord Torphichen and later they were owned by the Mures of Caldwell. This family supported the Covenanters (opponents of Charles I's innovations in Church of Scotland worship) in the seventeenth century although Capelrig for a short time was in the hands of General Tam Dalyell who was a supporter of the Royalist cause. In 1765 the Capelrig estate was purchased by Robert Barclay who was a lawyer in Glasgow. He built the mansion seen here. Eastwood High School, Newton Mearns, was built on the Capelrig estate and opened in 1864. In 1962 the house became a community centre after being in a neglected condition for almost forty years and has been a council office building since 2004.

Cardell House

The mansion of Cardell was situated on rising ground above Wemyss Bay, overlooking the River Clyde. It was built in the Scottish Baronial style with Tudoresque and Jacobean details. This view dates from about 1915. Cardell was formerly the home of Sir William Pearce, Bart. (1833 – 1888). He trained as a shipwright and naval architect at Chatham Dockyard and in 1863 moved to Scotland where he became surveyor to the Lloyd's Register on the River Clyde. One year later he was appointed general manager of Robert Napier and Sons where he designed transatlantic liners for the Compagnie Générale Transatlantique. In 1869 he became a partner in John Elder and Company and by 1878 was the sole owner of this firm. In 1886 it became known as the Fairfield Shipbuilding and Engineering Company with Pearce as chairman. This firm was one of the most prominent shipbuilding companies in the world. Pearce was also Chairman of the Guion Line of Steamers and the Scottish Oriental Steam Shipping Company. He was Conservative MP for Govan and was awarded a baronetcy, and after his death in 1888 his estate was valued at £1,069,669. Cardell has been demolished and the site is now occupied by a block of flats.

Cartsburn House

Cartsburn House was built in the seventeenth century. According to a report on the property in 1856, the date 1672 could be seen inscribed above one of the windows. It was situated on high ground near Greenock but the house was demolished and the site is now occupied by later buildings. Cartsburn House was the principal residence of the Barons of Cartsburn. Thomas Crawfurd was created first Baron of Cartsburn in 1669. In that year he obtained a Crown charter in confirmation of one which had been granted 36 years before, whereby the lands of Cartsburn were erected into a burgh of barony. The estate of Cartsburn incorporated the lands of Cartsdyke, or Crawfurdsdyke, and a portion of the lands of Easter Greenock Castle. Thomas Watt, grandfather of the inventor James Watt, was a former Bailie of the Barony of Cartsburn and the Burgh of Barony of Crawfurdsdyke. The poet Robert Burns resided at Cartsburn House at the invitation of Thomas Crawfurd, fourth Baron of Cartsburn. Cartsburn School was later erected on the site of the house but it was completely destroyed during the Greenock Blitz in 1941.

Castle Semple House

The Sempill family originally occupied a castle on the site of Castle Semple House and was associated with this area from the fifteenth century. In 1727 the estate was sold by Hugh, eleventh Lord Sempill, to Colonel William MacDowall and this house was built for him between 1735 and 1740. This classical mansion was located on the north-west side of Castle Semple Loch. The route to the property from the west was through the West Gates at Lochwinnoch and then down a long drive which was situated between the estate plantations and the lochside. William MacDowall obtained plans from the famous architect, Robert Adam, to make alterations to the mansion in 1791 but these did not take place because of the financial problems experienced by the family. The condition of the property deteriorated and the sale of estate lands began in 1808. In 1814 the house was acquired by Major John Harvey and in 1908 the Harveys sold the estate, which was divided into a number of smaller holdings and Castle Semple House was converted into apartments. In 1924 it was gutted as a result of fire and was finally demolished in the mid to late 1960s. All that remains is a house conversion of its most easterly wing.

Castle Wemyss

Castle Wemyss at Wemyss Bay was originally a mansion which was built about 1850 for Charles Wilsone Brown. He sold it to John Burns in 1860 and he appointed Robert William Billings to remodel the mansion in the Scottish Baronial style. Billings enlarged the property with the additions of a new floor, new wings and a clock tower. Burns was in control of the family business of G. and J. Burns, shipowners, from 1860 and later he was a partner and chairman of the Cunard Steamship Company. In 1890 Burns succeeded to his father's baronetcy and seven years later was created first Baron Inverclyde of Castle Wemyss. The castle had many important visitors and these included the social reformer Anthony Ashley-Cooper, seventh Earl of Shaftesbury, the author Anthony Trollope, King Peter the Second of Yugoslavia and Emperor Haile Selassie of Ethiopia. Castle Wemyss was the property of the Burns family until the death of John Alan Burns, fourth and last Baron Inverclyde in 1957 (the title became extinct as he had no heirs). After the fourth Baron's death no member of the family was able to afford the upkeep of the castle and the estate was sold in the 1960s. Inverkip Power Station was built in the estate grounds in 1970/71; this was the only oil-fired power station ever built in Scotland. Castle Wemyss was demolished in 1984 and all that remains is a flagpole and some rubble. A housing estate was constructed on the site in the 1990s.

Cowden Hall

Cowden Hall estate, at the north-western edge of Neilston, has a long history dating back to the twelfth century. The Spruil family owned a castle here and the land for a considerable period of time. Walter Spruil was Lord Chief Justice to Malcolm, Earl of Lennox, in 1294. The castle was no longer in existence by the sixteenth century but a laird's house was built in the eighteenth century and is still standing. Cowden Hall was a nineteenth century mansion built for Robert Orr after he sold the nearby Crofthead Mill in 1859 to R.T. and J. Alexander. The estate was then redesigned and trees from all over the world were planted there. In the grounds of this imposing mansion there were croquet lawns, tennis courts, a bowling green, a boating pond and boathouse. There were also extensive greenhouses and a large conservatory. The Crofthead Mill was owned by the English Sewing Cotton Company from 1898. A total of 1,500 workers were employed in the mill in the first decade of the twentieth century. These workers enjoyed the amenities of the estate which also included a billiard hall and a venue for dances. The mansion was used as a convalescent home for soldiers during the First World War. It was demolished in 1962 and the Crofthead Mill ceased operations in 1992. Residents of Neilston now have access to the estate.

Craigends House

Craigends House was situated two and a half miles north-east of Kilbarchan, near the south bank of Gryffe Water. In 1857 the old Craigends House was rebuilt and extended by David Bryce R.S.A into a particularly fine example of Scottish Baronial architecture. The lands of Craigends were granted to William Cunninghame in 1479. He was the first Laird of Craigends and his descendants were lairds until the twentieth century. Alexander Cunninghame, sixteenth Laird, lived in his new property until 1866 when he died aged 62. John Charles Cunninghame then inherited Craigends at the age of fifteen. He was the last laird, dying without an heir in 1917. His wife, Alison, lived in the mansion until her death in 1958 when the property was inherited by a nephew. In October 1961 there was an auction of the house's contents, after which time the building became unoccupied. Over the next decade it fell into a state of disrepair with most of the roof disappearing and the floors collapsing. In 1971 most of this magnificent property was demolished and only the front entrance was left in position. It was finally demolished in 1980. Considerable housing development has since taken place on the site.

Crookfur House

This is a view of Crookfur House in Newton Mearns, taken about 1910. Until the 1950s it was the home of the Templetons who were a branch of the well-known carpet manufacturing family. Crookfur House and grounds was described by Alan MacCallum, gardener to the Templetons between the first and second world wars in the following terms: '[It] was a charming old mansion clad in front with ivy . . . the windows looked out on to a pleasant lawn and the planted grounds around were studded with hardy trees among which were fine groups of rhododendrons.' There was also a flower garden, a walled garden, two small orchards, a peach house, a vinery, a fig house and a fernery. In the 1950s Crookfur House was sold and for a short time it was a hotel. Later it was seriously damaged by fire and then demolished. In 1964, the Linen and Woollen Drapers' Association, having purchased the estate, commissioned Sir Basil Spence, Glover and Ferguson to design a housing scheme for people who had retired from the drapery trade. The original accommodation consisted of fifty cottages and some self-contained flats. The building of the cottages was completed in 1967 and they were formally opened by Lady Fraser of Allander on 27 September of that year. This complex with added accommodation is now known as the Retail Trust Crookfur estate.

Crookston Castle

Crookston Castle is situated on a small hill in the Pollok district of Glasgow, five miles south-west of the city centre. The lands of Crookston were purchased by Sir Alan Stewart of Darnley in 1330. His descendants replaced Sir Robert de Croc's original timber and earth structure with the present castle about 1400, although retaining the original surrounding defensive ring-ditch. The Stewarts of Darnley were Earls of Lennox from 1425. In 1489 the forces of King James IV attacked the castle using the famous Mons Meg cannon. The result was that the western end of the castle was almost completely destroyed. Several decades later, in 1544, the Earl of Arran and Cardinal Beaton's forces besieged and took the castle. In 1757 the then owner of the castle, William Graham, second Duke of Montrose, sold the property to the Maxwells of Pollok. In 1931 Crookston Castle was the first property which was acquired by the National Trust for Scotland. It was presented by Sir John Stirling-Maxwell, tenth Baronet of Pollok, who was a founder member of the Trust and later its president from 1943 until his death in 1956. Crookston Castle is still owned by the National Trust but is maintained by Historic Scotland.

Dargavel House

At the beginning of the sixteenth century the lands of Dargavel came into the possession of John Maxwell. Dargavel House was built by his descendant, Patrick Maxwell, in 1584. It was constructed in the French style which was introduced during the reign of Mary, Queen of Scots, in the mid-sixteenth century. There is an armorial stone dated 1584 in the east gable of the mansion which confirms the date of its erection by the Maxwells. The property was extended and altered in 1670. A north wing was added to Dargavel House between 1849 and 1851. This was designed by David Bryce who was Scotland's most famous Victorian architect and responsible for perfecting the Scottish Baronial style. After fire damage in 1909, interior restoration work was undertaken by Peter Macgregor Chalmers. Dargavel House was acquired by the Ministry of Defence in 1937 along with a number of neighbouring farms prior to the construction of the Royal Ordnance Factory in Bishopton. The last owner of the property was Captain Alexander Hall-Maxwell who was a descendant of the two ancient Renfrewshire families of the Halls of Fulbar and the Maxwells of Dargavel. The final occasion on which the garden and grounds of the mansion were open to the public was on 12 May 1937 when a garden fete was held to celebrate the Coronation of King George VI. The lands of the former Royal Ordnance Factory are currently being developed for housing on a very large scale. Dargavel House, about one mile south of Bishopton Station, remains in position.

Duchal House

The history of the lands of Duchal, a short distance south-west of Kilmacolm, can be traced to the thirteenth century when the Lyle family was in possession of Duchal Castle, of which some remains still exist. The Lyles were a powerful family in the locality and also in the nation. In 1488 Robert, Lord Lyle, was appointed Lord High Justiciar of Scotland by King James IV after the Battle of Sauchieburn, and James resided at Duchal Castle on a number of occasions. The estate was purchased by John Porterfield in 1544 and after that time the castle fell into a ruinous condition. His descendant, Alexander Porterfield, built a new house in 1710. This building now forms the south range of Duchal House which was extended eastward by Boyd Porterfield in 1768. The estate and mansion passed to Sir Michael Robert Shaw-Stewart, seventh Baronet, in 1855. In 1913 Duchal House was purchased by Joseph Paton Maclay who was created a Baronet in 1914 and elevated to the peerage as the first Baron Maclay in 1922. He was Chairman of Maclay and Macintyre, shipowners. He also held office as Minister of Shipping in the coalition government of David Lloyd George during the First World War. A prominent member of the Maclay family was John Scott Maclay, Secretary of State for Scotland from 1957 until 1962 and created first Viscount Muirshiel in 1964. He was the fifth son of the first Baron Maclay. The Maclay family still reside in Duchal House, which is considered to be one of the finest mansions in Renfrewshire.

Elderslie House

Elderslie House was situated near the south bank of the River Clyde, a short distance from Renfrew. The building of this property took place between 1776 and 1782 and it was built for Alexander Speirs who was the main partner in the Glasgow banking firm of Speirs, Murdoch and Co. He was also one of the founders of the Glasgow Arms Bank. Speirs became a very rich man and purchased over 10,000 acres in Renfrewshire. However, he only lived in Elderslie House for a few months after its completion, dying in December 1782. That same year the historian William Semple described the mansion in the following terms: 'Mr Speirs has built an elegant large modern house about 40 yards north from where the old Inch Castle stood being 90ft. long and 60ft. broad, and four storeys high with a pavilion roof having a platform covered with lead on the top.' Fellow historian George Robertson referred to Elderslie House as a building of 'palatial proportions'. The Speirs family resided in the property until the death of Captain Archibald Alexander Speirs, the great-grandson of Alexander Speirs. The house was demolished in 1924 and Braehead Power Station and various factories were later erected on its site and grounds.

Erskine House

The estate of Erskine belonged to the Erskine family from the end of the twelfth century. The first known proprietor of the estate was Henry de Erskine in 1226. Walter Stewart, sixth Lord Blantyre, purchased the estate from William Hamilton in 1703/04. His descendant, Robert Walter Stewart, eleventh Lord Blantyre, began the building of Erskine House in 1828 but it was not completed until 1845. The stone used in the construction came from a quarry on the estate. Charles Walter Stewart, twelfth Lord Blantyre, inherited Erskine House from his father. He married Lady Evelyn Leveson-Gower, daughter of the second Duke of Sutherland. Their only son and heir, the Hon. Walter Stewart, Master of Blantyre, died in 1895 as a result of a riding accident and the twelfth Lord Blantyre died in 1900, leaving the house to his grandson, William Arthur Baird. It was bought by Thomson Aikman in 1912 and a short time afterwards he sold it to John Reid who later received a knighthood. Reid gifted Erskine House plus 360 acres of estate for use as a hospital for wounded servicemen who had served in the First World War. The first patients were admitted to the hospital on 10 October 1916 and it was officially opened on sixth June 1917 by HRH Princess Louise, Duchess of Argyll. It was originally known as the Princess Louise Hospital for Limbless Sailors and Soldiers, but was later renamed Erskine Hospital. In 2000 the facility was relocated to two new locations, one of which is on the site of the house's nursery gardens. The house itself had a £15 million restoration and is now an exclusive hotel known as Mar Hall.

Finlaystone House

The Dennistons (originally Danielstouns) were associated with Finlaystone from 1296. Sir Robert Danielstoun died in 1399 and his daughter Margaret inherited the estate. She married Sir William Cunningham of Kilmaurs in 1405 and his grandson Alexander Cunningham was created Earl of Glencairn in 1488. This family owned the Finlaystone estate until 1796 when John, fifteenth Earl of Glencairn, died unmarried. Thereafter the mansion and estate were in the possession of the Cunninghame-Grahams until 1863. In that year the new owner was Sir David Carrick-Buchanan who later sold Finlaystone House to George Jardine Kidston in 1897. The house has been the home of the MacMillans since 1929 when Marion Blackiston-Houston, granddaughter of George Kidston, married Gordon Holmes Alexander MacMillan (later General Sir Gordon). Their son George Gordon MacMillan inherited Finlaystone in 1955 and his son, Arthur MacMillan, is the current owner. The building of a new mansion on the south bank of the River Clyde near Langbank, took place in 1764 the architect being John Douglas. The north wing of this new property incorporated what remained of the fifteenth century castle. In 1900 George Kidston commissioned Sir John James Burnet to redesign the mansion in the Scots Baronial style, completing the work in 1903. Since 1975 the estate, with its extensive gardens and woodland, has been open to the public.

Fore House

The Georgian mansion of Fore House is situated in Locher Road, Kilbarchan, and was built in 1773 for John Barbour Jnr, also known as John Barbour of Law. His father was Bailie John Barbour (1701 – 1770) who was the first member of the family to become a weaving merchant and bleacher in Kilbarchan. The Barbour family supplied flax in the form of spun yarn to weavers in the locality, then collected the woven material for bleaching and marketed the finished textiles. Apart from his business activities, Bailie Barbour was active in the local community as a Justice of the Peace, treasurer of the parish church and also an elder. John Barbour Jnr seems to have had a large factory in Kilbarchan and, like his father, was also active in the life of the village. In 1785 when the heritors (landowners) and the local kirk session met in order to discuss the issue of the fund for the poor in the parish, he was appointed Preses (chairman or president). He traded with Dublin and also had business connections in Ulster, and he and his descendants made a significant contribution to the linen trade which resulted in the establishment of large mill complexes in Ireland, England and the USA. As a result of the business activities of the Barbours, Kilbarchan became well known for its successful weaving trade in the nineteenth century.

Gallowhill House

In 1864 Peter Kerr of Clark and Company, threadmakers in Paisley, purchased the estate of Gallowhill and built Gallowhill House in 1867. It was designed in the French Baronial style by William Forrest Salmon (1843–1911) of the Glasgow architectural firm James Salmon and Son. It was considered to be one of the finest mansions in the district and was situated in a dominant position near what is now Priory Avenue in Gallowhill, Paisley, but nothing now remains of it. Peter Kerr's thread-making company was formerly Underwood Mill before merging with Clark and Company. This mill had the first James Watt-designed steam engine in Scotland in 1799. Peter Kerr's daughter Elizabeth Anne married the future Sir Hugh Houston Smiley in 1874. Many years later Lady Smiley presented Gallowhill House for use as an auxiliary hospital for soldiers who had been wounded in the First World War. She also provided funds for the Hugh Smiley day nursery in memory of her husband who died in 1909 and there are a number of Hugh Smiley nurseries in Paisley today. Sir Hugh Houston Smiley had the original idea for the nursery as he had a great interest in the welfare of children. He was created the first Baronet Smiley of Drumalis (in Larne, Co. Antrim) and Gallowhill, Paisley, in 1903.

Garthland House

Garthland House near Lochwinnoch was built in 1796 by David King for landowner James Adam. The property was formerly known as Garpel House and then Barr House before becoming Garthland House. It was later extended between 1820 and 1830 by William MacDowall of Garthland. The MacDowalls originally came from Wigtownshire where the family had owned the lands of Garthland since the thirteenth century. The first mention of the MacDowalls being in Renfrewshire was in 1727. William MacDowall, who died unmarried in 1810, was the first member of the family to be described as Laird of Garthland and Castle Semple. In 1936 Garthland House became St Joseph's College which was under the auspices of the Mill Hill Foreign Missionary Society. The college provided education for boys who had a vocation for the priesthood in the area of foreign mission work. A three-storey dormitory block was built in 1936 and this was linked to the mansion. A chapel was built in 1943 and it also served as a place of worship for local Roman Catholics until a chapel was constructed in Lochwinnoch in 1955. St Joseph's College closed in that year and the building was converted into St Joseph's Nursing home which operated until 2004. Since that time the condition of the former Garthland House has deteriorated and it has become derelict and neglected. Planning permission has been given to build flats on the site.

Glen House

The Glen was situated on high ground from where Stanely Castle could be seen. The site of the mansion today is beside the children's play area in Glen Park, Paisley. The Glen was originally part of the barony of Thornley and has been owned in former times by the families of Wallace, Blair, Abercorn and the Cochranes of Dundonald. The mansion was built about 1859 for William Fulton. He owned the dyeing and finishing works which were nearby. This factory was known as Glenfield Scouring Works which was established in the 1820s as a bleachworks. Later, it was William Fulton and Sons Ltd. This firm ceased operations in 1966. It was famous throughout the country for 'Glenfield Starch' which the firm claimed was the only starch used in the household of Queen Victoria. William Fulton's first job was a weaver and although he became a rich man he did not forget his origins. When he came into possession of the Glenfield estate he expressed a desire 'that all the people of Paisley would be at liberty to come and walk by the braes and glens, as if it were their own'. William Fulton also organised annual concerts on the estate with a choir of about 700 members composed of mill girls and other female workers from Paisley. In their heyday the audiences at these concerts numbered an amazing 30,000 people. There was no equivalent to these concerts elsewhere in Scotland and they were similar in scale to modern pop festivals. The concerts took place from 1874 until 1936 and raised funds for charitable purposes.

Glencoats House

The building of Glencoats House in Paisley was completed in 1890. It was designed by Hippolyte J. Blanc and was situated on the other side of the railway line from Ferguslie House and near Ferguslie Mills. Blanc later designed two extensions to the house. This property was the home of Thomas Glen-Coats who was the son of Thomas Coats of Ferguslie and Maxwelltown and Margaret, daughter of Thomas Glen of Thornhill, Renfrewshire. Thomas Glen-Coats was born at Ferguslie House in 1846 and was educated at Queenwood College in Hampshire. Thomas was chairman of the famous thread manufacturers J. and P. Coats. In conjunction with J. and P. Clark, this firm constituted the largest thread-manufacturing business in the world. Thomas Glen-Coats was Honorary Colonel and former Commandant of the second Volunteer Battalion of the Argyll and Sutherland Highlanders. In 1894 he was created the first Baronet of Ferguslie Park. He was Liberal MP for West Renfrewshire from 1906 to 1910 and held office as the Lord Lieutenant of Renfrewshire from 1908 to 1922. Sir Thomas's son, also Thomas, succeeded to the baronetcy when his father died in 1922. Sir Thomas, second Baronet, had no heir and the baronetcy became extinct after his death in 1954. Glencoats House was given to the old Royal Alexandra Hospital in 1934 for use as an auxiliary hospital. The donors, who also provided the finances for an endowment fund, were Sir Thomas Glen-Coats, second Baronet, Mrs E.H.T Parsons and Harold Glen-Coats. This auxiliary hospital closed in 1972 and was demolished in 1980.

Glenlora House

Glenlora House is situated one mile to the west above Corsefield Road, Lochwinnoch, in an elevated position 500 feet above sea level. There are extensive views of the nearby countryside from the mansion, which was built in the Tuscan style about 1840. It has a twin-columned porch, widespread eaves and a pedimented attic tower. The first owner of the property was John Buchanan and in 1865 he sold the mansion and estate to John McEwan, a partner in the firm of R. and J. Henderson, merchants in Glasgow. The Glenlora estate formed part of the Barony of Glen which in past centuries belonged to the Glens of Barr. The name of the mansion is derived from a glen on the estate which was originally contained within the lands of Langyards. Those lands were owned by the Orr family for a considerable period of time. The separate Glenlora estate dates from around 1818 when Langyards was in the possession of Robert Orr. The present estate consists of about 113 acres with landscaped gardens and wooded grounds. In recent years Glenlora House has undergone a massive transformation from a comfortable family home to one of the finest preserved small country houses in Scotland. This photograph of the mansion was taken about 1913.

Glentyan House

This mansion in Burntshields Road, by Kilbarchan, was built by Alexander Speirs in 1781. The mansion and estate were purchased in 1818 by Captain James Stirling, who was a naval officer. He first married his cousin Mary, who was the daughter of Day Hort Macdowall of Castle Semple. She died in 1839 and five years later Captain Stirling married Elizabeth Christian who was the daughter of James Dundas of Ochtertyre and widow of William Macdowall of Garthland. She was also one of his cousins. Soon after Captain Stirling acquired Glentyan House he began to purchase Old Master paintings and his collection became one of the best in Scotland. The captain was active in the public life of Renfrewshire and was appointed Deputy Lieutenant of the county in 1848. Thomas Mann, a Glasgow merchant, purchased the Glentyan estate in 1874 and in the 1880s prevented the villagers of Kilbarchan from walking on the long-used footpath which went through the estate. Two Kilbarchan weavers, Andrew Brodie and Malcolm Neil, took the case for reopening the footpath to the Court of Session in Edinburgh and won. However, Thomas Mann appealed to the House of Lords and was granted permission to block the footpath through his estate but only on condition that he provided an alternative right of way, to which Mann agreed. Two later owners of Glentyan House were Richard H. Hunter and Sir Reo Stakis.

Two young men pictured on the putting course in the grounds of Gourock House. In 1784 Duncan Darroch (1740 – 1823) purchased the lands and barony of Gourock from the Stewarts of Castlemilk after having made his fortune in Jamaica. Gourock House was built near Gourock Castle which had been demolished about 1747. The house was acquired by Gourock Town Council in 1923 and was later demolished. The site was donated to the town of Gourock by the Darroch family. The land was originally known as Darroch Park and later renamed Gourock Park. In 1847 Lieutenant General Duncan Darroch (1774 – 1847), grandson of Duncan Darroch, erected the tower on Tower Hill and was responsible for building the square tower on the present Old Gourock and Ashton Parish Church. The present head of the Darrochs of Gourock is Claire Darroch-Thompson. In 2011 she succeeded her father, Duncan Darroch of Gourock, and in the same year she was Chieftain of the Gourock Highland Games. In so doing she followed her father, grandfather and grandmother who presided over the event from 1956 until 1983.

The first owner of Greenbank House was Robert Allason who was a baker and later became a trader with his brothers in Port Glasgow. He amassed considerable wealth by trading in tobacco and slaves with Britain's American colonies and also acquired land in the Caribbean. His wealth enabled him to purchase Flenders Farm in 1763 (his ancestors had worked on this farm for centuries) and it was on this land that the sixteen-room Greenbank House was built a short time afterwards. The property is located in Clarkston, about six miles from Glasgow city centre, and has had several owners in the two centuries following its construction. In 1962 it was purchased by William P. Blyth who, with the assistance of his wife, designed the present ornamental gardens. Prior to their arrival the grounds had mainly been used for growing fruit and vegetables. In 1976 the Blyths gave the house, its two-and-a-half-acre walled garden and sixteen acres of the estate to the National Trust for Scotland. The garden has about 3,000 plants which blossom throughout the changing seasons and the Trust has described it as an 'educational garden to inspire and educate visitors on what and how to grow a very wide range of more unusual plants which are available in the trade.'

Haggs Castle

Haggs Castle is located in the Pollokshields district of Glasgow two and a half miles south-west of the city centre. A heraldic panel above the original main door indicates that the castle was built in 1585 for Sir John Maxwell of Pollok and his wife, Margaret Cunningham. This property was built to replace a previous castle of the Maxwells which was formerly on the site of the present Stables Courtyard in Pollok Country Park. The Maxwells ceased to reside in Haggs Castle after the building of Pollok House was completed in 1752. Thereafter the property fell into disrepair and it was not until a century later that restoration work took place. At that time it was owned by Sir John Maxwell, eighth Baronet. Further work on the castle was undertaken in 1899/1900 when a drawing room and a billiard room were added on the north side of the property. On the south side a circular staircase and a new entrance were also constructed. A Mr J.C. Murray rented Haggs Castle from the beginning of the twentieth century until 1930 after which time there were a number of tenants until the early 1940s. In 1943, during the Second World War, the castle was taken over for military purposes. At the conclusion of hostilities it was divided into four apartments which were available for rent until 1972. In that year the Corporation of the City of Glasgow purchased the property which later became the Museum of Childhood. It was formally opened by John Craven of the BBC in 1976 and closed in 1997. Haggs Castle is now a private residence.

Houston House

Houston House is situated one mile north-east of Bridge of Weir and just north of the village of Houston. Houston Castle was originally located near the present mansion. It was a sixteenth century courtyard castle which was formerly in possession of the Earls of Lennox. In 1780 James Macrae bought the Houston estate and demolished three sides of the courtyard when he made alterations to the castle. Alexander Speirs of Elderslie then purchased the estate two years later. He had made a fortune as a tobacco merchant and was one of the wealthiest of the Glasgow tobacco lords. The present west wing of the mansion (formerly the Palace Wing of the old castle) was in a derelict and roofless condition until the 1830s when it was redesigned as a shooting lodge. In 1872 the architect David Thomson designed a new mansion south-east of the older building. At that time many of the old outbuildings were demolished. Additions to the west and east of Houston House were made between 1893 and 1895 and these were also designed by Thomson. The Speirs family were owners of the Houston estate for five generations. Major David Makgill-Crichton-Maitland was the owner of Houston House from 1959 until 1995 when it passed to his son Mark Crichton-Maitland. Major Makgill-Crichton-Maitland was Lord Lieutenant of Renfrewshire from 1980 to 1994. Houston House has now been divided into six separate apartments.

Johnstone Castle

Johnstone Castle was originally known as Easter Cochrane and was built around 1600. The lands of Johnstone were acquired by Sir Ludovic Houston in 1645. He gave these lands to his second son, George, who became the first Houston laird of Johnstone. The castle was purchased by the Houstons in 1733. Additions were made to the property in 1771 with further alterations taking place in 1812 when it was changed to a castellated design. There were more alterations to the upper parts of the castle later in the nineteenth century. A famous visitor to the castle in 1848 was the Polish composer, Frédéric Chopin, who had previously given music tuition to the wife of Ludovic Houston, the fifth laird. George Ludovic Houston was the last laird to reside in the castle. During the Second World War the property was acquired by the War Office and a prisoner-of-war camp was built in the grounds. In 1950 the castle became vacant and apart from the tower, the entire building was demolished. Johnstone Burgh Council acquired the site in 1956 in order to build council houses. Reworking of the remaining structure was carried out in 1958. At present, all that remains is the central square tower and a crow-stepped bartizaned section of an earlier period. It is now surrounded by a housing estate on Tower Road, Johnstone.

Jordanhill House

The Jordanhill estate was formerly located in the parish of Renfrew and Jordanhill House was built in 1782 by Andrew Houston. Archibald Smith (1749 – 1821) purchased the house in 1800 and made a number of additions to the property. He had amassed a fortune in trading with the West Indies and also held office in Glasgow as Lord Dean of Guild. His son, James Smith (1782 – 1866) modernised the interior of the house. He was a Fellow of Trinity College, Cambridge, and became a Fellow of the Royal Society as a result of his geological investigations, and the house was later inherited by his son, Archibald Smith (1813 – 1872), a lawyer who also achieved great distinction by compiling the Admiralty Compass Manual in collaboration with a Captain Evans. As a result he received the gift of a gold compass from the Emperor of Russia and was also awarded the Gold Medal of the Royal Society of which he became a Fellow. Jordanhill House along with sixty acres of land was acquired by the Glasgow Provincial Committee for the Training of Teachers shortly before the First World War as a site for a new teacher training college. The mansion provided a home for Belgian refugees during the First World War and later served as a student hostel for Jordanhill College which opened in 1922. The mansion was demolished in 1961 and two years later the Crawfurd Building was erected on the site, which later became part of the University of Strathclyde. It was named after Thomas Crawfurd who had built a house at the same location in 1562.

Kelly House

Kelly House was built two miles south of Inverkip for Alexander Stephen of Linthouse in 1890 after the previous mansion on the site was demolished. The architect was William Leiper and it was a very large and ornate mansion with tall chimneys and turrets, and there were also extensive landscaped gardens. It was destroyed by fire on 5 December 1913 (see the front cover). West Renfrewshire Fire Brigade was called to the fire at 5.39 a.m. on that day but the flames were not extinguished until 10 p.m. Some 2,200 feet of hose had to be used. The cost of the damage was estimated to be £15,000, a considerable sum at that time, and while the cause of the fire was never fully discovered it is thought that it might have been started by suffragettes. The ruins of Kelly House remained standing until the 1940s and the estate was divided and sold in the 1950s. There is now a caravan park on the site of the house. The lands of Kelly have a long history and were granted to the Bannatyne family in the latter part of the fifteenth century. This family built Kelly Castle which was burned down in 1740. John Wallace, a West Indies trader and tobacco merchant, owned the estate from 1792 and built a plain white mansion which stood until the late nineteenth century. It was enlarged by his son, Robert Wallace, who served as the first MP for Greenock from 1833 to 1845, and subsequent owners of the mansion before it was replaced by the new house were James Scott and Dr James Young F.R.S. who founded Young's Paraffin Light and Mineral Oil Company in 1865.

Langside House was designed by the distinguished Scottish architect Robert Adam (1728 – 1792) and was built in 1777 on the crest of the hill between Mansionhouse Road and Camphill Avenue, quite near the present Mansionhouse Gardens in the Langside district of Glasgow. The first owner of the house was Dr Thomas Brown who had become wealthy after working in London. In 1775 he had become a partner in the Ship Bank, then based in Glasgow, and the following year he bought the 100-acre estate as the site for the mansion at a cost of £4,000. The house was described by the historian William Semple in the following terms: 'An elegant large modern house upon an eminence, three stories high, pavilion roofed, with a platform covered with lead'. The property was inherited successively by three of the four sons of Thomas Brown; the third son, also Dr Thomas Brown, sold the house to Neale Thomson who owned the Camphill estate. He was responsible for developing a feu plan which resulted in the building of villas and terrace houses for professional and business people who wished to reside in what was then a rural location. Langside House later became a preparatory school for St Aloysius' College which was founded in 1859. The mansion was demolished in the 1950s.

Linwood House

A. B. Stevenson, Linwood

Seen here around 1908, Linwood House was situated in Napier Street, Linwood. It was built for the Watson family who owned the town's paper mill. Robert and William Watson took over the Linwood Cotton Spinning Mill in 1872 and established a paper manufacturing business there. Watson's became famous for their Linson paper which was invented in 1936 in the mill laboratory. This was a binding material for books and the name 'Linson' is a combination of 'Linwood' and 'Watson'. The former London County Council was the first major organisation to use Linson paper for binding its books and W.H. Smith followed their example. Watson's exported Linson paper to fifty countries. The firm also made a wide range of paper for industrial purposes and this included paper for Jacquard looms in the textile business. By 1970 R. and W. Watson were the largest manufacturers of paper-based bookbindings in the world. The last owner of Linwood House was Brian Hick in 1970. He operated a coach hire business. Hick sold Linwood House which was subsequently demolished and the site is now occupied by private housing.

Linn House

Left: This mansion was built in the 1820s on part of the lands of Hagtonhill by Glasgow shipping merchant Colin Campbell, who used it as a summer residence. These lands formerly belonged to the Maxwells of Pollok. Campbell's property was named The Lynn after the waterfall on the White Cart Water and he planted much of the woodland in the estate. In the 1840s John Gordon of Aitkenhead purchased the Lynn estate and in 1852 added a side extension to the mansion which was designed by the architect Charles Wilson. In 1919 the Corporation of the City of Glasgow purchased the estate, amounting to 180 acres, for £10,000 and from that time the estate was known as Linn Park. A further eighteen acres of the lands of Cathcart Castle were added to the park in 1927 and the four-acre area known as Court Knowe was added in 1933. Of Glasgow's parks, only Pollok Country Park covers a larger area. The Lynn is now known as Linn House and underwent a conversion into four apartments in 2006/07. It is thought that John Gordon of Aitkenhead planted the Lime Tree Avenue which runs through the park.

Right: Merchiston House was built in 1880 and was located near where the village of Brookfield is now situated. With its distinctive round tower, this mansion was known locally as 'The Castle'. The Finlayson family, who were a branch of the linen-thread manufacturers Finlayson, Bousfield and Co., occupied the property until the late 1930s. This firm established the Barbush Mill in Johnstone in 1849. The firm later became part of the Linen Thread Co. Ltd but this went out of business in the late 1950s. Merchiston House was used as accommodation for Canadian soldiers during the Second World War. In 1945 it was purchased by the Burgh of Paisley for use as a hospital for people with learning difficulties, becoming Merchiston Hospital which was taken over by the National Health Service in 1948. Redevelopment of the hospital began in 1979 with the construction of four 30-bed cottages for patients. In January 1985 a new complex was opened, consisting of more cottage units, education centres, therapy and recreational units and costing almost £9 million. The following year the former Merchiston House was demolished amidst opposition from residents in nearby Brookfield. Merchiston Hospital was closed in 2007/08.

Merchiston House

Milliken House

Milliken House near Kilbarchan was built in 1826 by Sir William John Milliken-Napier, eighth Baronet of Merchistoun. It replaced the previous mansion which had been destroyed by fire in 1801. In 1886 Sir Archibald Lennox Milliken-Napier, tenth Baronet, sold the estate and the mansion to Archibald Mackenzie who was a Paisley starch manufacturer. At that time the estate consisted of the village of Kilbarchan and eleven farms, amounting to about 1,564 acres. However, by 1921 when Mackenzie sold the estate it had been reduced to 447 acres. The new owner was George Arthur Boswell, a well-known architect who was President of the Glasgow Institute of Architects around 1930. Boswell demolished Milliken House and built a new property from the estate factor's house, stables and cart shed. He used much of the original stone from the former mansion. This building was Boswell's home and became known as the White House of Milliken which is situated in a small estate of 132 acres. The stone edifice of the Milliken-Napier arms is the only artefact left from Milliken House and is situated near the entrance of the main drive to the White House of Milliken.

Monkdyke House

Monkdyke House was built in Alexandra Drive, Renfrew, in 1897 for Colonel Walter Brown who was formerly head of William Simons and Company, Shipbuilders. In his will he directed that after the death of himself and his wife, the house should be presented to the Burgh of Renfrew for use as an art gallery and museum. Colonel Brown died in 1924 and his wife in 1942, but on 13 March 1941 Monkdyke House was partially destroyed by German incendiary bombs. As a result of this damage the property was left derelict and roofless for some years. Renfrew Town Council wished to rebuild the house and applied for compensation under the War Damage Act but as it was to be a museum this compensation could not be paid. The result was that in order for the building to be restored, an arrangement was made between the government and the town council of Renfrew to have Monkdyke House rebuilt as the council chambers. On 29 December 1951 Monkdyke House was officially opened as such by John W. Gibson, Provost of Renfrew. Prior to this time council meetings took place in Renfrew Town Hall. Monkdyke House no longer serves as the council chambers; it has been extended and altered and is now a sheltered housing complex managed by Renfrewshire Council.

Mossend House

Right: The substantial mansion of Mossend was in the possession of the Crawford family until the early years of the twentieth century. This is a photograph of the property from about 1904. It is now much altered and is no longer a family home. Mossend was built facing onto both Barr and Castle Semple lochs on the main road leading into Lochwinnoch. Around 1966 this property was purchased by Agnes McNeil who was a businesswoman in Paisley. She converted it into the Mossend Hotel, which was later owned by John Wilson, a local dairyman. In 1989 further conversion work took place at the hotel. An extension was added to the left of the property and a patio terrace was constructed at the front which overlooked a children's play area. Whitbread Inns invested almost £1 million in the purchase and refurbishment of the hotel, reopening it in 1989 as the first 'Brewer's Fayre' in Scotland. In 2003 it became the Hungry Monk Restaurant.

Muirshiel House

Left: Muirshiel House was situated 700 feet up in the foothills of Misty Law. It was used as a shooting lodge and is thought to have been built in the mid-nineteenth century by businessman John Millar. By the mid 1870s the owner was Francis Conyngham, second Marquess of Conyngham. Gilbert Thompson Bates is recorded as owning the estate in 1910. His daughter Mary married the next owner, Sir Edward Lionel Fletcher. He was greatly interested in shooting and with assistance from various gamekeepers and estate workers made Muirshiel one of the best sporting estates in Scotland. The estate was offered for sale in 1935 at £8,500, comprising the house, 3,300-acre estate, 1,000-brace grouse moor, river and loch fishing, two sheep farms and a number of cottages. On 24 June of that year the estate was purchased by Bernard Fitzalan-Howard, third Baron Howard of Glossop. In 1939 part of the estate was sold to the local authority and in 1944 a further portion was sold to Kerr and Cawdor Ltd. Colonel Bill Stirling, the managing director of that firm, was the last occupant of Muirshiel House, residing there from 1945 until 1950. The mansion house was demolished in 1952, the same year that Kerr and Cawdor Ltd sold the estate to Renfrewshire County Council. Muirshiel Country Park, which was created in 1970, is now located on the estate.

Netherhill House, Paisley, was built in 1856 for Robert Roger who was a local procurator fiscal. The architect of this property was Charles Wilson. John Baird of Harvey's wine and spirit merchants, acquired Netherhill in 1865 and the Clark family owned the mansion from the 1880s to the 1890s. This family became famous for the development of thread manufacturing in Paisley. They discovered a method of producing a spooled thread and were the first firm to manufacture it at their Anchor Mills. In 1906 the owner of Netherhill House was William Young of the dredger building company of Lobnitz in Renfrew. Thirteen years later the property was acquired for the Society of the Sisters Faithful Companions of Jesus and it became St Margaret's Convent. This convent had been previously situated in East Buchanan Street, Paisley. A school was built in the grounds of the convent and this was later taken under local authority control. In 1978 the Sisters of St Margaret's Convent left Netherhill House and moved to a smaller house in Riccartsbar Avenue in St Mary's Parish, Paisley. Netherhill House later became derelict and was demolished in 1982.

Newark Castle is located in Port Glasgow on the south bank of the River Clyde. The site was owned by the Denniston family but became part of the Maxwell estate in 1402 when Elizabeth Denniston married Sir Robert Maxwell of Calderwood, Lanarkshire. George Maxwell built the tower house and gate house in the late fifteenth century and a famous early visitor to the castle was King James IV in 1495. In 1597 Patrick Maxwell redesigned the property with both interior and exterior alterations and in 1668 George Maxwell sold some of the land surrounding the castle to the City of Glasgow in order that a new port could be established for trading purposes. This area was originally named Newark. William Cochran purchased Newark Castle in 1694. In the 1820s it was owned by Robert Farquar who was a banker in London. His daughter married Sir Michael Shaw-Stewart whose family owned the property until 1909. None of these owners lived in the castle and it was leased to various tenants. However, the property was in a ruinous condition by 1909 when it was taken into state care and partial restoration took place. It is now in good condition and is managed by Historic Scotland. Newark Castle is considered to be one of the best examples of a Scottish sixteenth-century building to survive.

Pollok Castle

Pollok Castle was a mansion situated one mile west of Newton Mearns. The site was the property of the Pollok family from the twelfth century. In the grounds there is a motte which is possibly the original residence from that time of Fulbert de Pollok, the founder of this family line. Pollok Castle was built in 1696/97 and incorporated a fifteenth century keep which is the main tower or fortified building of a castle. In these years Sir Robert Pollok was responsible for the construction work. He demolished the east and south walls of the old keep and used what remained for the south-west corner of the property. Pollok Castle was severely damaged by fire in 1882, after which restoration work took place. In 1947 the castle was demolished and all that remains are its foundations. The property occupied a site above the valleys of the rivers Clyde and Cart from where there were views over a wide expanse of countryside. It had four storeys with highly decorative stonework. In the gardens there were features such as sundials, pavilions and ornate gateways.

Around 1269 Sir John Maxwell became the first knight of Pollok and his descendants continued to live at Pollok until the twentieth century. Pollok House was built between 1747 and 1752 and was designed by William Adam. There are thought to have been three previous castles on the estate. Sir William Stirling-Maxwell (1818 – 1878), ninth Baronet, was a great collector of Spanish art and in 1848 his *Annals of the Artists of Spain* was published in three volumes. His son, Sir John Stirling-Maxwell, modernised the property, resulting in the installation of electric lighting, extra bathrooms, improved kitchen facilities, more bedrooms and an extensive service quarter in the basement. Part of the Pollok estate was made open to the public from 1911 and the house was utilised as an auxiliary hospital during the First World War, with wards in the billiard and dining rooms. The inaugural meeting of the National Trust for Scotland took place in 1931 in the Cedar Room. In 1966 Sir John's daughter, Mrs (later Dame) Anne Maxwell Macdonald, gave Pollok House along with 361 acres of parkland to the City of Glasgow. There were terms made in this gift to provide a site for the Burrell Collection although it was not until 1983 that the building housing the collection was formally opened by Her Majesty the Queen.

Polnoon Lodge

Polnoon Lodge was built in 1733 as a hunting lodge for Alexander Montgomerie, thirteenth Earl of Eglinton. The family's main residence had been the fourteenth-century Polnoon Castle until the beginning of the sixteenth century when they moved to Eglinton Castle in Ayrshire. The property in this photograph dates from the late eighteenth century and is located in Polnoon Drive, Eaglesham. In 1844 the whole of the Eaglesham estate was sold to Allan and James Gilmour and Polnoon Lodge was briefly the estate office before being occupied by Allan Gilmour's mother and sisters until the 1860s. In the 1920s it was a temperance hotel which meant that no alcohol was sold. Later it served as a boarding house. By the 1960s Polnoon Lodge had been abandoned but Renfrew County Council carried out restoration work, converting it into flats for the elderly which received a Civic Trust Award in 1971. There is a house in Cheapside Street, Eaglesham, which is in effect Polnoon House in miniature.

Ralston House was designed by David Hamilton in 1810 for William Orr, a Glasgow merchant, although an older part of the mansion had already been built in 1797. In 1864 extensions to the property were added for the then owner, Thomas Richardson, from designs by Campbell Douglas. The house was demolished in 1934. Two lodges which were the original gate houses survive as private residences and are located in Glasgow Road, Paisley. Ralston Golf Club now occupies the site of the former mansion and the converted stableblock is the club house. During the First World War Ralston House was known as the Red Cross Hospital for Paralysed Sailors and Soldiers. It continued to serve as a convalescent home for ex-servicemen until its demolition. The Ralstons were an ancient Renfrewshire family and Nicolaus de Ralphstoun is recorded as appearing as a witness to the grant of lands of Fulton by Sir Anthony Lombard to the monks of Paisley in 1272. It is thought that the name Ralston originated in a 'Ralph' or 'Ralf' who is said to have been a son of one of the Earls of Fife. He came to Renfrewshire where he obtained lands, naming them 'Ralfstoune' or 'Ralstoune'. The Ralstons owned these lands until 1704. They were then held successively by John, Earl of Dundonald, Lady Anne Cochrane, the fifth Duke of Hamilton and the MacDowalls of Castle Semple. William MacDowall sold the Ralston estate to William Orr in 1800. These lands were divided up and sold as farmland in the late nineteenth century.

Scotstoun House was built at the beginning of the eighteenth century by William Walkinshaw of Barrowfield. In 1748 it came into the possession of Richard and Alexander Oswald. Extensions to the property were made in 1825 from designs by the architect David Hamilton for Elizabeth Oswald (1767–1864) who was the owner at that time. Scotstoun House had a total of 49 separate rooms which included wine cellars, a nursery and two large libraries. This is a view of the property from 1870, showing its setting in open parkland. Scotstoun House was demolished in 1893 and later that year the Lanarkshire and Dunbartonshire Railway Company was granted a compulsory purchase order over the land occupied by the mansion for a railway line between Stobcross and Clydebank. The mansion was located to the south of Dumbarton Road, Glasgow, near where Ardsloy Place is situated. A 'new' Scotstoun House was built 100 yards west of the site of the old mansion, on the slopes of Scotstoun Hill. This property was contained within the Scotstoun estate, which amounted to about 1,000 acres immediately west of Partick on the land between the River Clyde and Great Western Road. The second Scotstoun House was demolished in 1962 and its site is now occupied by the Kingsway high-rise flats.

Southfield House

The ivy-covered Southfield House in Newton Mearns, pictured in the early years of the twentieth century. The Southfield estate has a long history and formed part of the Barony of Mearns. In 1491 King James IV confirmed these lands in the possession of John, Lord Maxwell, and his wife, Agnes Stewart, Lady Maxwell. In 1530 the Barony of Mearns was granted by King James V to Beatrix Douglas, daughter of the King's half-sister and James, third Earl of Morton, although the Southfield estate was retained for Lady Maxwell who was by then a widow. At a later period the Barony was acquired by the Stewarts of Blackhall. The Southfield estate was sold in 1691 by Sir Archibald Stewart of Blackhall to Robert Urie of Millbrae. Alexander Hutchison, a Jamaican merchant, acquired the estate in 1771 and Hugh Hutchison inherited Southfield about 1813. After his death it passed to his only child, Charlotte, who married Sir Thomas Montgomery-Cunninghame, eighth Baronet of Corsehill in 1832. He died in 1870 but Lady Montgomery-Cunninghame remained resident until 1902. In 1913 the Southfield estate was purchased by the Corporation of the City of Glasgow. The house was demolished shortly after the end of the First World War and in 1930 Mearnskirk Hospital for children with tuberculosis was opened on the site by the Corporation's Public Health Department.

Stanely Castle

The Barony of Stanely originally belonged to the Dennistoun family, granted by King Robert I in 1312 to Sir Robert Dennistoun. After his death it came into the possession of his daughter Elizabeth who was married to Sir Robert Maxwell of Calderwood. Stanely Castle is thought to have been constructed in the early fifteenth century. In 1629 John Maxwell sold the castle to Dame Jean Hamilton, widow of Robert, fourth Lord Ross of Hawkhead. It later passed by marriage to the Boyle family in the middle of the eighteenth century. This family experienced serious financial problems and the castle was abandoned and fell into a ruinous condition. In 1837 George Boyle, fourth Earl of Glasgow, sold the building and lands to the Paisley Water Company. The surrounding marsh was flooded in order to create a reservoir to supply Paisley with water and Stanely Castle has been partially submerged since that time. Philip Ramsay in his *Views of Renfrewshire* of 1839 recorded that in the eighteenth century there was a schoolroom in the low vaulted apartment at the north-east corner of the castle, where local children were taught reading, writing and arithmetic. Stanely Castle is a typical fifteenth-century tower house. An extension was made in the sixteenth century. Its four floors included a kitchen with a huge fireplace, a great hall, bed chambers for the family and accommodation for servants.

Thornliebank House (The Mansion House), Rouken Glen

The area of Rouken Glen Park was originally known as the Birkenshaw estate, which was purchased by Walter Crum (1796 – 1867), a chemist and businessman who became a Fellow of the Royal Society in 1844. His eldest son, Alexander Crum MP (1828 – 1893), rebuilt the Mansion House which was also known as Thornliebank House. He also designed a walled garden for the property and carried out planting in the existing woodland. After his death it came into the possession of his brother William who sold the mansion and estate to Archibald Cameron Corbett MP (later first Lord Rowallan) in 1905. The next year Corbett presented the mansion and estate to the citizens of Glasgow and Rouken Glen Park was formally opened to the public on 25 May 1906. During the Second World War Thornliebank House was used for military purposes. Later, its condition deteriorated and it was demolished in 1963. There was a proposal to close Rouken Glen Park in 1983 which met with great disapproval. However, as a result of negotiations between the Glasgow and Eastwood local authorities the park was leased to the then Eastwood District Council (from 1996 East Renfrewshire Council) for 125 years from 16 June 1984.

Tower Rais

The mansion of Tower Rais was built in 1870 and was later occupied by the Montfort Fathers. The Montfortian Religious Family derives its origins from St Louis-Marie Grignion de Montfort (1673 – 1716), a French priest who was canonised by Pope Pius XII in 1947. The Montfort Fathers ceased residing in Tower Rais in 2006. This mansion in Darnley Road, Barrhead, has since undergone complete renovation and has been converted into luxury apartments. There was a previous Tower of Rais which was located half a mile north of Barrhead. It was built between 1437 and 1449 by the Stewarts of Darnley and was later known as Stewart's Rais. This was a small square tower with thick walls which was later used as a hunting lodge. It was partly demolished in the early decades of the nineteenth century in order to provide material for houses in the locality and the structure was finally removed in 1932, the stones being used for road construction. Rais is an old Scots word which means 'rise'.

The Scottish patriot Sir William Wallace (c.1270 – 1305) is thought by some to have been born in Elderslie but not in Wallace's Buildings, seen here around 1913, which are the remains of the seventeenth-century Wallace Farm. Elderslie was property of the Wallace family from the thirteenth century until about 1850. These buildings at 243 Main Street were demolished in 1973/74 and some foundations are all that remain. William Wallace became a prominent leader in Scotland against the English during the Wars of Independence. He achieved a victory at the Battle of Stirling Bridge in 1297 and from 1298 he was Guardian of the Realm in the name of John Balliol (King of Scots, 1291 – 1296). Wallace was later caught by the English and executed in London. The Wallace Memorial in Elderslie was designed by John G.T. Murray and J. Andrew Minty and erected in 1912.

Railways in Cumbria
Compiled by David Spaven

ISBN 978-1-913893-20-0

First published in 2022 by Transport Treasury Publishing Ltd. 16 Highworth Close, High Wycombe, HP13 7PJ
Totem Publishing, an imprint of Transport Treasury Publishing.

www.ttpublishing.co.uk

Printed in Tarxien, Malta By Gutenberg Press Ltd.

'*Railways in Cumbria*' is one of a series of books on specialist transport subjects published in strictly limited numbers and produced under
the Totem Publishing imprint using material only available at The Transport Treasury.

Front Cover: Ivatt Class 2 2-6-0 light mixed traffic loco No. 46426 shunts Flusco lime works south-east of Blencow station in an undated shot thought to have
been taken during the mid-1960s when the loco was based at Carlisle Upperby shed. The loco is known to have been in immaculate condition for working a June
1964 railtour between Penrith and Workington, so this shot may have been taken shortly thereafter. The rail-connected works was established in the mid-1930s; it
also had an extensive narrow-gauge railway system with its own wagons and locomotives. 46426 entered service (at Bescot) in 1948 and was withdrawn in 1966,
but seven members of the class have been preserved, including 46441 on the Lakeside and Haverthwaite Railway in south Cumbria. *Neville Stead Collection*

Frontispiece: On 13th April 1965, ex-Midland Railway Fowler Class 4F 0-6-0 No. 43964 powers the 2.35pm Egremont-Ullcoats Mine trip along this West
Cumberland branch (see also images 71-73), with a train mostly composed of 16T mineral wagons (capable of being emptied by tippling at the steel works) rather
than similar tippler wagons devoid of the side doors specifically built for the movement of iron ore. In the 1950s the Ullcoats Mine (incorporated in 1897) was
connected underground to the nearby Florence Mine, which was already served by its own short branch line, but the Ullcoats Mine and branch survived until
around 1968, as did the Florence Mine branch which became redundant on the closure of Millom Ironworks in September of 1968. 43964 was finally withdrawn
from service, at Workington, just four months after this shot. *Larry Fullwood*

Back Cover: Ex-LMS Ivatt 4MT 2-6-0 Class No. 43000 draws the lightweight 6.32pm Langholm-Carlisle train into Riddings Junction on 6th April 1963. 43000 was
the first of this class of 162 locomotives to be delivered - in December 1947, only weeks before nationalisation - and had a working life of just under 20 years,
being withdrawn from service at Blyth (North) in 1967. It had been based at no fewer than eight sheds, including Carlisle Upperby, Canal (at the time of this photo)
and Kingmoor between 1961 and 1966. One of the class survives in preservation, on the Severn Valley Railway. The passenger station at Riddings closed together
with the Langholm branch in June 1964 (one of the earliest Beeching closures in Scotland), with freight succumbing in January 1967.

Introduction

Even in today's rationalised railway world, Cumbria – England's most north-westerly county – offers a microcosm of what the iron road does. And the variety was all the greater in the heyday of the railway, shaped by a distinctive geography and major economic forces in the form of mass tourism and concentrated industrial development. In his comprehensive history of the railways of the Lake Counties, David Joy writes of how: ". . . in the space of a few hundred square miles [the Lake District] contains England's highest mountains, largest concentration of natural lakes and most dramatic scenery. It undoubtedly forms the dominant influence on the Lake Counties as a whole, a clearly defined region embracing Cumberland, Westmorland and the detached portion of Lancashire north of Morecambe Bay, since 1974 administratively united in a single county which adopted the ancient Celtic name of Cumbria."

Add to the mix a lengthy coastline indented by estuaries and rivers such as the Coniston, Derwent, Duddon, Eden, Esk and Kent – and a strategic position en route from London to Glasgow – and you have a recipe for a glorious railway geography and history.

Many fine books have been written about the railways of Cumbria – and the region is eminently well-served by the publications of the estimable Cumbrian Railways Association – so this photo album does not seek to rival such detailed accounts of the ins and outs of railway engineering and operations over the last 175 years. Rather we have selected 81 photos from the substantial Transport Treasury archive which illustrate the character of many of the lines which served (and some which still serve) the Lake Counties – and we have sought to provide some unusual images from locations which have often been bypassed in the (literal and metaphorical) rush along the West Coast Main Line over Shap. But the latter has not been neglected either.

The album is organised around distinct railway centres or 'corridors', and within each of these the photos are generally placed in chronological order. We begin with Carlisle and then work broadly clockwise around the system. The modern boundary of Cumbria has largely defined our limits, with the notable exception of a modest incursion into Lancashire at Carnforth, still a key gateway to the county's railways.

The earliest of our photos dates back to 1939, and the most recent to 1970, but the very large majority capture scenes in the 1950s and 60s, the last years of steam and the first of diesel. In many cases we have been able to credit the individual photographer, but in others (where the term 'Collection' is used) their names are sadly not known.

Very much known to me, however, is our cartographer, Alan Young, who has illustrated most of my books (and the Disused Stations web site); Alan hand-drew the delightful map of Cumbrian railways overleaf. Given the span of time covered by the photos, I deliberated for some while over a suitable snapshot year for the map to depict the extent of the Cumbrian rail network. In the end I chose January 1954, which pre-dates by a few months the first significant post-war closures of freight lines in West Cumberland as part of the long drawn-out decline of the local iron and steel industry.

Industrial decline (and the rise of road transport) had long previously impacted on passenger rail services in West Cumberland – with significant route closures in the 1930s – but it would not be until 1958 that Cumbria saw the first line (Coniston) to lose post-war all its passenger services. The region then suffered from Dr Beeching's 1963 prescription, with the Lakeside, Workington-Keswick-Penrith and Silloth lines all lost in the 1960s and 70s, and the Windermere branch severely rationalised. But it could have been so much worse, as the Beeching Report also advocated closure of the southern section of the Cumbrian Coast Line, from Whitehaven to Barrow, and the Settle & Carlisle line came perilously close to closure in the 1980s. We can therefore still enjoy many of the scenic delights of Cumbria's railways from a train, while indulging nostalgia for past times in this album.

Acknowledgements and sources

I am particularly grateful to my old friend, fellow rail campaigner and railway history aficionado, Bill Jamieson, for his detailed knowledge of locomotive and operations history and associated input to virtually all the photo captions – and his help with selecting photos from the Transport Treasury archive. Other important sources of intelligence included:

- A Regional History of the Railways of Great Britain Volume 14: The Lake Counties, by David Joy (David & Charles, 1990)

- https://www.brdatabase.info/

- https://www.railuk.info/

- LMS Engine Sheds Volumes 1 and 4, by Hawkins and Reeve (Wild Swan, 1981 and 1984)

- various Journals and books of the Cumbrian Railways Association

- Wikipedia.

David Spaven
Edinburgh, October 2021

David Spaven has spent his working life in and around the rail industry, and for 20 years was a campaigner for the re-opening of the Borders Railway. He is the author of 10 books in the last decade, including two award-winners: Mapping the Railways and Highland Survivor: the story of the Far North Line. His 11th book – Scotland's Lost Branch Lines, an in-depth analysis of the Beeching era – was published by Birlinn in March 2022

Glossary
To avoid repetition of company names etc in full in the map captions, a short glossary is provided below:

BLS — Branch Line Society

LMS — London, Midland & Scottish Railway

LNWR — London & North Western Railway

LYR — Lancashire & Yorkshire Railway

MLS — Manchester Locomotive Society

MR — Midland Railway

SLS — Stephenson Locomotive Society

WCML — West Coast Main Line.

Map
Not all freight-only lines – nor all lines closed completely – are marked. The only remaining passenger services on the Kirkby Stephen East to Tebay line were summer Saturday advertised trains between the North East and Blackpool and unadvertised fortnightly trains between Durham and Ulverston (for miners to convalesce at Conishead Priory). The line from Moor Row through Egremont to Sellafield is shown as open to passenger traffic, as unadvertised workmen's trains continued to serve these locations.

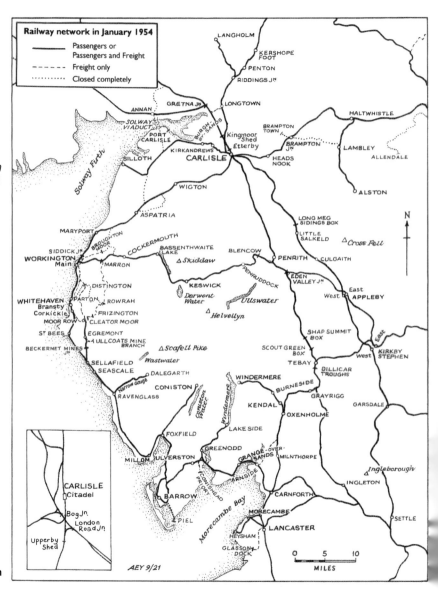

1. Streamlined LMS 'Coronation' Class Pacific No. 6227 Duchess of Devonshire awaits departure from Carlisle Citadel station with the northbound 'Royal Scot', which the Camden-based loco will have worked throughout between London and Glasgow. 6227 entered service in 1938, and the clean but not pristine paintwork evident here suggests that this undated photograph was taken in the summer of 1939, prior to wartime exigencies. Designed by William Stanier, a total of 38 'Coronations' were built at the LMS Crewe Works between 1937 and 1948. Locos were based at a variety of locations along the WCML, with 6227 being shedded at Carlisle Upperby in 1946-47 then Crewe North and Polmadie in BR days. The entire class was withdrawn between 1962 and 1964. *Neville Stead Collection*

2. Framed by the imposing train shed, Workington-based Fowler 2P Class 4-4-0 No. 40694 awaits departure from the Maryport line bay platform at the south end of Carlisle Citadel station. The photo is undated, but the early BR 'blood and custard' coaching stock livery suggests the early to mid-1950s - certainly no later than May 1955 when the loco moved south to Preston. This class (built between 1928 and 1932 at Derby and Crewe for light passenger work) was an LMS development of a 1912 Midland Railway design and in the 1950s could be found across the old London & North Western Railway system, the south-west of Scotland and the former Somerset & Dorset line. The last members of the class, including 40694, were scrapped in 1962. *Neville Stead Collection*

3. A classic railway backcloth at Carlisle Upperby in 1957 as ex-LMS Class 3F 0-6-0T No. 47666 brings a transfer freight from the north side of the city off the ex-London & North Western Railway (LNWR) Up goods line. The train consist, which the 'Jinty' will shortly propel into the marshalling yard, includes a container in a conventional open wagon, a van, and steel bars on bogie bolster wagons. The LMS rebuilt Upperby engine shed in 1948, replacing the original shed with a large concrete roundhouse (out of shot to the right) and this might have been expected to survive as a modern traction maintenance depot. In the event, and despite main-line diesels being based here from 1959, the shed closed completely at the end of 1966. Today only a few sidings remain here. *Neville Stead Collection*

4. A fine array of traction is admired by enthusiasts at the south end of Carlisle station on 5th September 1959. On the far left is ex-LMS 'Jubilee' Class 4-6-0 No. 45729 *Furious* on an Up WCML express. The adjacent centre road is occupied by English Electric Type 4 No. D211, which will probably replace 45729 in a few minutes time. Named *Mauretania* the following year, D211 was one of the first 'production' as opposed to 'prototype' Type 4s, and had entered service only a few months earlier. 'Black 5' No. 45029 sits in the other centre road, and to her right is Haymarket-based ex-LNER Class A3 No. 60096 Papyrus - named after the 1923 Derby winner - which has brought in the Up 'Waverley' service from Edinburgh to St Pancras. *Mike Mitchell*

5. Ex-North British Railway (NB) D34 'Glen' Class No. 62484 *Glen Lyon* sits light engine in the centre road at the north end of Carlisle station, no doubt prior to working the 6.13pm stopping train to Hawick, a regular duty during its year's sojourn there, which ended in November 1961. To the left, in the bay platform, is ex-LNER A3 Class Pacific No. 60093 *Coronach* arriving on the 2.36pm service from Edinburgh Waverley due in Carlisle at 6.0pm - note the 'E' (for Eastern Region) numbered leading coach on an internal Scottish Region service. Built in 1928, Coronach was based at Carlisle Canal shed from 1941 until withdrawn in 1962. To the right on through Platform 3 sits an unidentified 'Coronation' Class Pacific, recently arrived on a terminating WCML passenger service. *Neville Stead Collection*

6. Tender-first ex-LMS Ivatt Class 4 2-6-0 No. 43028 passes Bog Junction in Carlisle on what looks to be a transfer freight from one of the pre-Grouping yards on the south side of the city, probably London Road, to one on the north side, ie before the opening in 1963 of Carlisle New Yard at Kingmoor. The junction was located on the avoiding lines which kept goods traffic passing through Carlisle away from the Citadel Station corridor. This through avoiding route was severed following a runaway Freightliner train accident in 1984, but Bog Junction (controlled from Carlisle Power Box) remains as the point where freight spurs from the WCML and from east of Carlisle come together prior to joining the Maryport Line at Currock Junction. *Neville Stead Collection*

7. 'Black 5' No. 44790 powers a parcels train north from Carlisle towards Scotland over the Eden Viaduct, just south of Etterby Junction and Kingmoor MPD. The northern approach to Carlisle was largely rebuilt in preparation for the 1877 opening of the goods avoiding lines to the west of Citadel station, effectively creating a quadruple track WCML through the city from Upperby Bridge Junction in the south to Port Carlisle Branch Junction, visible in the far distance of this undated shot. The pressure of wartime traffic forced the LMS to provide an additional two tracks between the latter and Etterby Junction in 1942, hence the modern reinforced concrete viaduct on the right. 44790 was based at Kingmoor shed from late 1953 through to withdrawal in early 1967. *Neville Stead Collection*

8. On a dull day in the mid-1960s, an unidentified 'Britannia' Class Pacific passes London Road Junction box shortly after leaving Citadel station with a stopping service for the Settle & Carlisle line. The first railway here was the Newcastle & Carlisle's Canal branch (1837) followed some nine years later by the sharply curved line (seen on the left) of the Lancaster & Carlisle Railway to a very temporary terminus at London Road - hence the LNWR style signal box at this location. For most of its life this curve has served as a freight-only south to east chord, but today its main function (now as a single-track railway) is turning steam locos off terminating charter trains arriving in Carlisle from the south. *W.A.C. Smith*

9. Strictly speaking this delightful scene is not in Cumbria, but the train is en route to the county, at Alston! Veteran ex-North Eastern Railway Class G5 No. 67241 tackles the gradient out of Lambley station in an undated shot prior to this loco's 1955 withdrawal from service, after a working life of almost 61 years. Lambley station (opened in 1852) was in a magnificent setting with a fine view of the sandstone viaduct taking the railway across the River South Tyne. The station building and the viaduct survive to this day, and the South Tynedale Railway hopes to extend the line from its current terminus at Slaggyford through Lambley to a Haltwhistle interchange with the Newcastle-Carlisle railway. *Neville Stead Collection*

10. A lot of railway activity squeezed into a small space. Ex-LNER Class J39 No. 64812 sits at the 1,000 ft-high terminus of the Alston branch in an undated shot. The train shed is supported by the station building and covers the single platform and two tracks, and its west side is joined to the engine shed, a smith's shop and a water tower. Opened along with the branch in 1852, the engine shed was extended in 1873 and then saw useful service through to dieselisation of the passenger service in 1959. Slated for closure in the 1963 Beeching Report, the station lost its train shed in the mid-1960s, but the Haltwhistle-Alston service survived until 1976 due to inadequate local roads - and Alston station is now the base of the narrow-gauge South Tynedale Railway. *Neville Stead Collection*

11. Seen here in 1956 - with a Triumph TR2 sports car (perhaps the photographer's) parked adjacent - the station building at Alston is described in the Disused Stations website as 'an imposing Tudoresque structure of the East Coast main line type, with random stone courses instead of the more urbane ashlar, mullioned windows, moulded door and window hoods, ball finials, and lofty couple chimney stacks'. Despite final closure by BR in 1976 (the last rural closure stemming from the 1963 Beeching Report) both this building and the goods shed (just visible to the right) have survived, are Grade II-listed, and form integral parts of the narrow-gauge South Tynedale Railway operation, the shed now housing a museum. *Neville Stead Collection*

12. A fine head of steam is generated by K1 Class No. 62029 as it pulls away from Brampton Junction on an eastbound freight of chemical tanks and open wagons on 5th March 1960. Two tracks leading towards the former Brampton & Hartleyburn mineral line, which connected through to Lambley on the Alston branch and was operational until 1953, are still extant on the left. Prominent in the goods yard to the right are two 'Adcost' transit sheds, a design which was a fairly common feature of the railway landscape from the 1940s and 50s. The 2-6-0 K1 Class was a 1949 development of the Gresley mid-1930s Class K4 design and was chiefly associated with North-East England, all being withdrawn from service between 1962 and 1967. *Mike Mitchell*

13. Perth-based 'Black 5' No. 45473 shunts wrong-line - probably on an engineer's working - at Brampton Junction on 8th June 1965, looking east. To the right is the bare cutting of the lifted mineral-only Brampton & Hartleyburn Railway, while behind the camera to the left was the one-mile branch line to Brampton Town, a horse-drawn railway, opened to passengers in 1836 and closed as early as 1923. On the left, two vintages of railway goods shed are seeing little or no business, two years after the Beeching Report described both wagonload freight and less-than-wagonload sundries traffic as 'a bad loss maker'. However, Brampton passenger station (behind the camera) survives today as an unstaffed halt served by regular Newcastle-Carlisle services. *Henry Priestley (from Milepost collection)*

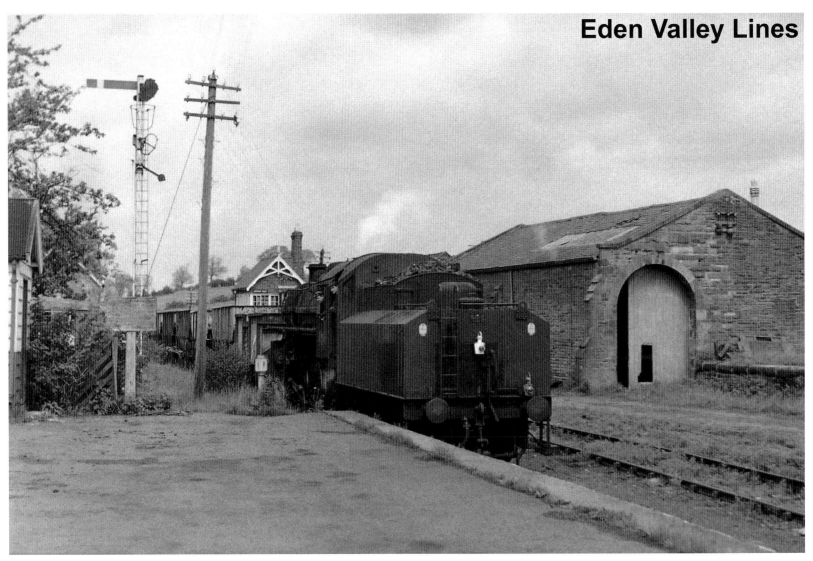

14. LMS-designed Ivatt 4MT 'Mogul' No. 43121 arrives at Appleby East station with the thrice-weekly trip freight from Carlisle Yard to Merrygill – sometime between June 1965 and November 1967 when the loco was based at Kingmoor. The station was opened in 1862 by the Eden Valley Railway (from Kirkby Stephen East to Eden Valley Junction on the WCML, thereby forming part of a through route from Penrith via Stainmore Summit to Barnard Castle and Darlington), which became a Stockton & Darlington Railway operation just a year later, in turn absorbed by the North Eastern Railway in 1864. Appleby East, which had only a single platform, saw freight operations continue until 1989, having been cut back in 1974 to Warcop military camp (six miles to the south east). It is hoped to restore heritage services over this section. *Norris Forrest*

15. Several period pieces are captured in this 1965-67 photo of Ivatt 4MT 2-6-0 No. 43121 shunting across the level crossing immediately north of (the ex-North Eastern Railway) Appleby East station. The Mogul locomotives, most of which were built by BR at Horwich Works, were noted (and criticised) for their American looks, in particular the running-plates positioned at a high level. The competition which had helped to close the railway to passengers is represented here by a Wolseley saloon sitting on the road which led south west to (the ex-Midland Railway) Appleby West station just a few hundred yards distant. The signal box and goods shed behind the signal box were subsequently demolished, but the station building (out of shot, to the right) remains in situ, and may yet see restored heritage passenger services. *Norris Forrest*

16. Kirkby Stephen East was served by the North Eastern Railway, but with nationalisation came under the control of BR London Midland Region. Here 4MT 'Mogul' No. 43121 arrives back at Kirkby Stephen East from Merrygill in a 1965-67 view looking west towards the once-extensive goods yard, with the closed passenger station beyond the masonry arch bridge. Kirkby Stephen had been a junction for 90 years, with lines north to Appleby and Penrith, east via Stainmore Summit to Barnard Castle, and west to the WCML at Tebay (all year public passenger trains to the latter being withdrawn in 1952). After the loss of the last passenger services here in 1962, track was lifted across the summit route but remained open to Hartley Quarry at Merrygill, just a few miles east of Kirkby Stephen, until 1974. *Norris Forrest*

17. Faded grandeur at Kirkby Stephen East in the last decade of the working railway, as 43121 pauses with a short train of hoppers on the sole remaining track, leading eastwards to Hartley Quarry. The station had a wide island platform with a 166 feet long train shed (overall roof), while there had also been a four-track engine shed out of shot to the right. Following the 1974 withdrawal of freight services, in 1996 the remaining former station building and land to the north were bought with a view to use as the eastern terminus of a proposed heritage railway from Appleby East. The Stainmore Railway Company and its volunteers have to date developed the site (including the train shed) as a heritage centre, with a short stretch of running line for passenger trips.
Norris Forrest

18. Not a photographic stance which would be permitted today! 'Black 5' No. 45236 has stopped for a 'blow-up' at Kirkby Stephen West on an Up freight in an undated shot sometime before the Carlisle Kingmoor-based loco's withdrawal from service in 1967. Neither the fine 'Upper Quadrant' semaphore signal on the left nor this signal box have survived. The former has been renewed using a much shorter tubular steel post, while the 1894 Midland Railway box was replaced in 1974 with one of standard London Midland Region design. At the time of the photograph the adjacent signal boxes would have been Crosby Garrett (to the north) and Mallerstang (to the south), both about three miles distant, and both now replaced by Intermediate Block signals. *Norris Forrest*

19. 'Black 5' No. 45253 battles up the 1 in 100 gradient through Kirkby Stephen West station on a southbound freight. The train consist includes Vanfits and a traditional wooden BD container displaying a 'door to door' logo. Kirkby Stephen lost its passenger services in 1970 but rejoined the network in 1975 as part of the 'Dales Rail' initiative. The scene is largely the same today, although the two semaphore signals have been renewed/moved and the Midland Railway signal box in the distance was replaced by BR - with parts relocated from Kendal on the Windermere branch in 1974. The station building (266½ miles from St Pancras) is now leased by the Settle and Carlisle Railway Trust, which comprehensively restored it to its original 'Midland Gothic' glory in 2009. *Norris Forrest*

20. In the first of a sequence of two undated shots, a BR Type 2 drifts past Long Meg Sidings signal box with a northbound fully fitted freight. This loco was from a batch constructed in 1963, confirming a mid '60s date for this and the next photograph. Meanwhile 'Black 5' No. 45364 has pulled a rake of empty wagons into the southernmost of the two loops, prior to picking up an adjacent rake of loaded wagons of anhydrite (for production of sulphuric acid, fertiliser and plaster). The nearby drift mine (behind the camera) was connected to the Midland Railway in 1886 and was closed in 1976 by British Plaster Board. The latter (as British Gypsum) still has a major rail-served processing plant for plaster at Kirkby Thore, some 10 miles to the south. *Norris Forrest*

21. No. 45364 has attached its rake of loaded wagons and is now heading north. In the background is Long Meg Sidings signal box, a BR London Midland Region design, which opened in 1955. Prior to that, access to the sidings had been ground-frame controlled and from the Up line only. Following the closure of the nearby mine in 1976, the box remained open as a block post for some years but was subsequently closed - leaving 15 miles between the remaining boxes at Culgaith and Low House Crossing (but split by Intermediate Block signals at Lazonby) - and eventually demolished in 2013 after decades of increasing dereliction. 45364 was built by Armstrong Whitworth of Newcastle in 1937 and based at Carlisle Kingmoor from 1963 until its 1966 withdrawal. *Norris Forrest*

22. 'Black 5' No. 45212 steams south past Culgaith station, level crossing and signal box with a diminutive goods train, in an undated shot thought to have been taken between 1965 and 1967 when the loco was based at Carlisle Kingmoor shed. The station - mid-way between Appleby and Langwathby - was not opened until 1880, and is noticeably not of the 'Midland Gothic' design seen throughout the Settle & Carlisle (S&C) line. It closed in 1970, but the level crossing and signal box survive to this day. 45212 was built by Armstrong Whitworth at Newcastle upon Tyne in 1935, and was one of the last steam locomotives to be withdrawn from BR service (in 1968). It was purchased directly from BR for preservation and is now based at the Keighley and Worth Valley Railway. *Norris Forrest*

23. This tranquil shot of Little Salkeld station, looking north, illustrates the 'Midland Gothic' architecture typical of the S&C - a style notable for distinctive weatherboarding and massive proportions. The station was opened in 1876, together with the line through to Carlisle, and closed in 1970 when BR withdrew local stopping services on the S&C. Unlike eight other stations on the line, Little Salkeld did not benefit from re-opening in 1975-76 as part of the 'Dales Rail' initiative - perhaps unsurprisingly, as Langwathby station is only 1½ miles to the south. Someone is just visible through the second window from the right, suggesting that this undated photo was taken shortly before closure. The station building is still extant, as a private residence. *Norris Forrest*

24. Carlisle Upperby based ex-Midland Railway Class 2P 4-4-0 No. 40356 gently simmers in the evening sunshine at Penrith engine shed, sometime between Upperby being coded 12A in mid-1950 and the transfer of the loco to Derby in early 1957. This loco was built to a Johnson design of 1883 but having been rebuilt twice by the MR there is little of the original (except for the tender) to be seen here. Surprisingly, the handful of 2P 4-4-0s at Upperby, including 40356, could still be found on WCML duties well into the 1950s, typically piloting overloaded or ailing class 6 locomotives ('Jubilees' and 'Clans') over Shap, and it is possible that the loco is on standby duty at Penrith rather than having brought in a local train from Carlisle. *Neville Stead Collection*

25. Class 6P 'Jubilee' 4-6-0 No. 45657 *Tyrwhitt* passes the impressive Shap Summit signal box with a northbound express, in an undated shot. At 916 feet high and approached by a gradient of 1 in 75 from the south, this was one of Britain's most challenging climbs in the steam era, typically requiring banking locomotives. 45657 was built at Derby Works in 1934 and was based at Carlisle Kingmoor from 1953 to 1961 - the maroon coaches and later BR emblem on the tender suggest that this scene was recorded towards the end of that period. There was a station at Shap Summit from 1923 until 1958, operated solely for the use of railway employees. The box was closed in 1973 when Carlisle Power Box took over. *Neville Stead Collection*

26. 4-6-2 'Princess Coronation' Class No. 46245 *City of London* forges uphill past Scout Green box, between Tebay and Shap Summit, with a northbound express - the direction of the sun and the ex-LMS brake composite coach behind the tender are consistent with this being the Keswick and Workington portion of the 'Lakes Express'. The loco still carries a 1B (Camden) shed plate, so the date can be no later than September 1963 - and July of that year, when the loco is known to have been running in immaculate condition (as here), seems likely. After barely a year at Willesden, 46245 was briefly at Crewe North prior to withdrawal in September 1964 - a total working life of just 21 years. Scout Green was a popular spot for photography - witness the gentleman on the right. *Neville Stead Collection*

27. 'Black 5' No. 44802 drifts down the 1 in 178 gradient through Oxenholme with a southbound freight train on 14th March 1964. Built by the LMS at Derby Works in 1944, 44802 was one of the last BR steam locos in service, being withdrawn at Bolton shed in 1968 and subsequently scrapped. Much has changed at this scene today - gone are the platform awning, water column, semaphore signals (including the short-armed starter signals), telegraph poles and the crossover from the WCML to the Windermere branch, while overhead wires frame the double track of the main line and the Down platform has been extended northwards. But Oxenholme remains an important railhead, as well as the junction for the last remaining branch in Cumbria, and the WCML is one of Britain's key arteries for freight traffic. *Larry Fullwood*

28. In an undated shot, 'Black 5' No. 45120 charges over Dillicar water troughs, with a rake of nine empty milk tanks (probably bound for Appleby and Aspatria) behind the loco, on a northbound Class 3 train mainly composed of parcels vans. Volume 14: *A Regional History of the Railways of Great Britain: The Lake Counties* describes the Dillicar experience thus: 'Trains thundering down Shap hit the troughs like an arrow in full flight, while northbound expresses made the most of the preceding favourable gradient to build up speed, and picked up water in a cacophony of smoke, steam and spray.' The troughs fell out of use with the end of steam in 1968, while 45120 (built at the Vulcan Foundry in Newton-le-Willows in 1935) was withdrawn from service at Carlisle Kingmoor shed in 1967. *Neville Stead Collection*

29. A visiting 9F 2-10-0, No. 92218 from Kingmoor, and three of Tebay's own stud of Standard Class 4 4-6-0 banking locos (all in less than pristine condition) sit at the utilitarian 1947/8 shed during the last few months of its working life. With its key roles as a base for banking locomotives up Shap and as the junction for the line to Kirkby Stephen and Darlington, Tebay generated a railway community with a population of around 700 by the turn of the 19th century. In 1960 the surviving freight operations to Kirkby Stephen ceased, and the final blows came in 1968 with the closure of the engine shed on 1st January that year, the cessation of banking duties from 6th May and the closure of the nearby passenger station on 1st July. *Neville Stead Collection*

30, 31 (top right) and 32 (bottom right). A series of three photos illustrates the taxing 7 mile long climb from Oxenholme to Grayrigg in the steam era. Taken from the bridge carrying the lane south from Grayrigg village over the WCML, seen here is an unidentified 'Black 5' hauling special freight 4Z63 banked by a Standard Class 4 4-6-0 towards the end of steam working to Carlisle in 1967. Of particular interest in the going away shot are the two 'Invacars' on flat wagons (the Invacar was a single-seater vehicle designed for use by disabled drivers, and distributed free by the government until the 1970s) and, just beyond the Grayrigg Down distant signal, the boarding where the footpath from Bank Houses to Hardrigg crosses the line. The banking loco will be Carnforth-based but outstationed at Oxenholme - the shed there had closed in June 1962 but the requirement for freights to be banked up to Grayrigg continued well past that date (passenger and parcels trains heavy enough to require assistance over Grayrigg and Shap were normally piloted throughout), indeed well into 1968 when No. 75027 of the type featured here performed the last banking duties on Saturday 4th May that year. *Norris Forrest*

33. Not in Cumbria, but controlling a sliver of its territory: the Caledonian Railway's Gretna Junction signal box controlled the WCML and the Glasgow & South Western Railway's main line where they converged just a few yards inside Scotland. The box seen here (west of the main line) came into service as late as 1915, taking over from both the former junction box nearby and the former Gretna Border Union Junction box to the south, where the NB chord to Longtown on the Waverley Route diverged. The NB line closed to passengers as early as 1915, and Gretna box itself closed in 1973, with its functions taken over by Carlisle Power Box. The 1915 structure was a classic Caledonian design with big overhanging eaves supported by curved brackets, and tall slender windows. *Norris Forrest*

34. Ivatt Class 2 No. 46491 sits at the head of a train from Penrith at Keswick's impressive station some time before the closure of the Keswick-Workington section in 1966. The 1951-built 46491 was based at Workington shed (12D) for most of its barely 16 year working life; given its grubby condition and the fact that DMUs had taken over the basic service in 1955, the working is likely to be the Keswick / Workington portion of the 'Lakes Express'. This named train (which was started by the LMS in the 1920s as a summer-only service from Euston to a host of destinations in the north-west) was withdrawn in 1965, one of the casualties of Beeching's scrutiny of summer holiday peak traffics (with rolling stock lying idle for much of the year) in his 1963 report. *Neville Stead Collection*

35. Keswick No. 1 box sits in a tranquil scene, looking east in halcyon BR days. To the left is the water tank supporting the attractive bracket of the water crane, while beyond that the station tracks converge into the single-line section to Threlkeld: the start of a 10-mile climb - much of it at 1 in 62½ - from 299 feet above sea level at Keswick to the line's 889 feet summit (a mere 26 feet lower than Shap). The 1967 rationalisation of remaining Keswick-Penrith branch infrastructure would remove all track bar that running by the box. Judging from the appearance of the Down platform, Keswick had an attractive station garden, perhaps one of the many which competed for 'Best Kept Stations' awards in the 1950s and '60s. *Norris Forrest*

36. A classic driver's eye-view of the west end of Keswick station, seen from the front of a Workington-Penrith DMU service: the signalman from Keswick No. 2 box awaits delivery from the driver of the single-line section token from Bassenthwaite Lake. In its prime the station had four platforms and attractive buildings with platform canopies: a fitting environment for the many visitors who used the line. The vans and other goods wagons in evidence indicate that this photo was taken prior to the cessation of goods traffic at Keswick in 1964. The imposing bulk of the Keswick Hotel (adjacent to the station) stands out in the middle distance, while small patches of snow on the distant fells - and bare tree branches - point to this being an early spring scene. *Transport Treasury*

37. Almost the same view as the previous shot, but taken from ground level - and now full of evidence of rail retrenchment (although a DMU can just be glimpsed between the two station buildings). Piles of coal remain in the goods yard, but now it arrives by lorry rather than train. The line west of Keswick closed completely in April 1966 and from December 1967 the branch from Penrith was operated as a 'long siding' and the remaining signal boxes closed. This shot is therefore likely to have been taken around this time. From July 1968 all five branch stations became unstaffed, no distinction being drawn between the minor intermediate stations and Keswick itself. The remaining branch closed in 1972, as one of the last of the Beeching-inspired cuts. *Norris Forrest*

38. Another view from the front of a DMU, looking east at Penruddock station - the only one on the line to have staggered platforms - with the Pennine range just visible between the ubiquitous telegraph poles. The east end of the station's crossing loop has been severed, suggesting a 1967/68 date for the photo. Despite the elimination of all loops, the switch from loco-hauled to more cost-effective DMU operation (as early as 1955), and latterly the destaffing of all stations, the combination of these economising measures was still not enough to save this scenic railway. But who can doubt that if it had survived, the Keswick branch would have been a popular and much-valued asset in the era of growing environmental concerns and summer road congestion in the Lake District? *Norris Forrest*

39. 'Royal Scot' class 4-6-0 No. 46143 *The South Staffordshire Regiment* sits at the head of a terminating passenger and parcels train at Windermere. 46143 sports a 9A (Manchester Longsight) shed plate - the loco was based there in 1952-53 and from 1955 to 1959, reinforcing the likely period of the shot suggested by the coaches on the right with their 'blood and custard' livery. Two of the three tracks in this shot were swept away in an over-zealous modernisation project associated with the electrification and resignalling of the WCML in the early 1970s. Subsequently the single track was cut back to a new truncated station to make way for a supermarket, which incorporates the facade and canopy of the original station. *Transport Treasury*

40. A steam era scene much changed today on Cumbria's only surviving branch line. Fairburn 2-6-4 tank No. 42299 pulls the 9.25am Windermere-London service out of Burneside station (opened in 1847) on 14th March 1964. Since 1973 the branch has been a 'long siding', with only the platform behind the train being still in use and passenger accommodation now comprising just a bus shelter - perhaps not unreasonable for a small town of around 3,000 inhabitants. 42299 was built for the LMS in 1947 and had a working life of only 18 years, its last stint being based at Carnforth from 1963 to 1965. The Windermere branch continued to be served by one return service on weekdays from Euston after dieselisation but this was discontinued from the timetable change in May 1970. *Larry Fullwood*

41. Stanier tank No. 42449 pauses at Kendal with the 8.10am Oxenholme-Windermere service on 14th March 1964. Built in 1936 at the LMS Derby Works, it had only eight months of working life remaining after this shot, being withdrawn from service at Carnforth in November 1964. The station's three platforms and impressive canopies, together with the ubiquitous parcels trolley - perhaps loaded with boxes of K Shoes, which would have constituted regular BR business - make for a scene little changed since the early days of the railway. Like the other stations on the branch, Kendal now has just a single platform - the one where the train is standing here - but fortunately the attractive station building on this platform has survived, albeit in non-railway use. *Larry Fullwood*

42. English Electric Type 4 No. D288 pulls the 8.10am Windermere-Manchester train - at least nine coaches long - away from Kendal on 14th March 1964. One of the products of BR's 1955 Modernisation Plan, this loco was delivered new to Crewe North depot in 1960, and had a working life of just 22 years - although one cab-end has survived in preservation at Crewe Heritage Centre. A year had elapsed since publication of the Beeching Report, but one wonders if anyone at Kendal that day could have predicted that just a decade later this scene would be utterly transformed? Only a single track remained and loco-hauled operation (unless 'topped and tailed') was history, but at least Beeching's proposal to withdraw stopping passenger services along the branch was rejected. *Larry Fullwood*

43. 'Britannia' Class 4-6-2 No. 70003 *John Bunyan* sits by Carnforth's gigantic coaling tower on Friday 8th July 1966. The chalked headcode 1M38 signifies the 14:00FSO Glasgow/Edinburgh to Manchester/Liverpool service, and it is thought that the 'Britannia' was booked to work through to Liverpool, so it may have failed en route and then gone on shed at Carnforth. 70003 had a working life of just 16 years, being withdrawn from service at Carlisle Kingmoor in March 1967 - so not quite surviving into the last summer of express passenger steam working over Shap. The reinforced-concrete coaling tower is today the last such structure surviving in Britain and forms part of the major operational base for West Coast Railways' charter services at the former 'Steamtown' heritage centre site. *Transport Treasury*

44. Ex-LNER Class K4 No. 3442 *The Great Marquess* hauls a rail tour returning from Ravenglass to Leeds past Carnforth East box on 10th September 1966. Introduced in 1938 for work on the West Highland Line, it began its long career in preservation - working on heritage railways and the main line - as early as 1961. After the expiry of its boiler certificate, The Great Marquess was displayed in the Museum of Scottish Railways at Bo'ness, and will eventually move to a museum in Fife, along with John Cameron's other engine, *Union of South Africa*. The chord over which the train is travelling here is no longer in use, while the surviving double-track of the Carnforth-Settle Junction line (foreground) is now controlled by Carnforth Station Junction box. *W.A.C. Smith*

45. BR 'Derby' Type 2 No. D7554 shunts mixed freight 7M92 from Hunslet at the north end of Carnforth yard on 23rd July 1968. The westernmost platforms of the passenger station - renowned for its role in the 1945 film Brief Encounter - can be seen behind the locomotive. What is less well known is that the lengthy platform canopy was the longest unsupported single-piece concrete roof in Britain when constructed in 1937. Just visible at the station is a Class 50 on the 16.10 Euston to Barrow, while the Corkickle to Northwich empty soda-ash hoppers stand adjacent in the yard. Built in 1965 and withdrawn in 1980, D7554 was one of a class of 327 1,250hp / 90mph locomotives, primarily designed for freight work, which became known as Class 25. *Arnold Battson*

46. On the fine evening of 9th May 1970, English Electric Type 4 (later Class 40) No. D353 awaits its scheduled 19.00 departure from Carnforth with 'Scottish Grand Tour No. 10' returning to Edinburgh. The excursionists traversed a high proportion of the surviving rail network in Cumbria that day, travelling out via the Settle & Carlisle to Hellifield, then to Ravenglass (using the Carnforth and Barrow avoiding lines) for a trip along the Ravenglass & Eskdale Railway. The homeward journey to Scotland was via Carnforth (where a visit was made to Steamtown). WCML main-line trains had ceased to call at Carnforth with effect from the timetable change the previous Monday, and this is believed to have been the last train to use the Down WCML platform. *Bill Jamieson*

47. At the 1923 grouping the LMS inherited 27 ancient Sharp, Stewart-built 0-6-0s from the Furness Railway. Ex-LYR Barton Wright 0-6-0s were soon sourced as replacements but these were hardly modern locos and by 1943/4 had given way to ex-LNWR 'Coal' and ex-MR Johnson 2F 0-6-0s - not exactly in the first flush of youth either. Barrow shed's allocation of the latter included No. 3412, seen here parked to the south of the shed building with the covered coaling stage on the right. While all had disappeared by nationalisation, there was clearly a need for lightweight 0-6-0s on local trip work and BR brought Johnson 2Fs back to Barrow in the early '50s, with the last one not leaving until 1963. The shed closed to steam at the end of 1966. *Neville Stead Collection*

48. An ex-LNWR Class 7F 0-8-0, recorded by the photographer as No. 49354, shunts Grange-over-Sands goods yard on 25th August 1953, three years before withdrawal from service. Originally built in 1903 as a 4-cylinder compound (LNWR Class B), No. 49354 was rebuilt to 2-cylinder simple form in 1921 (LNWR Class G1) and by the time of the photograph had been fitted with a higher pressure boiler, putting it in Class G2A. In 1857 the Furness Railway Company commissioned E.G. Paley - a Lancaster-based architect chiefly famous for designing, rebuilding and restoring churches, with most following the Gothic Revival style - to design the fine station building in the left background here; today it is Grade II listed. In 2012, the station as a whole was declared Heritage Station of the Year. *Henry Priestley (from Milepost collection)*

FURNESS RAILWAYS
CAUTION TO TRESPASSERS

Persons trespassing upon the railways belonging to the FURNESS RAILWAY company are liable to a penalty of FORTY SHILLINGS under the FURNESS RAILWAY act 1864 and in accordance with the provisions of the said act. Public warning is hereby given to all persons not to trespass upon the said railways.

AUGUST 1894.   BY ORDER.

ULVERSTON

49 & 50. Railway artefacts from two different eras. A Furness Railway trespass sign dated 1894 adorns a column on the side of Ulverston's station building, while a 1959 scene brings together a traditional gas lamp standard and a 'new' BR totem sign in London Midland Region maroon. In the distance is the Hoad Monument, a 100 ft high limestone tower resembling John Smeaton's Eddystone lighthouse, erected in 1850 to commemorate Ulverston-born Sir John Barrow (1764-1848) who was a founder member of the Royal Geographical Society. Alec *Swain / Norris Forrest*

51. By the time of this August 1959 shot from a passing train it had been 13 years since regular services had called at Greenodd, one of the three intermediate stations on the (Ulverston) Plumpton Junction-Windermere Lakeside branch, all of which closed many years before the branch itself. Passenger trains first called here in 1869, and for its new tourist line the Furness Railway had spared no expense on station buildings, using 'patent white bricks' - which were actually yellow - 'in a decorative and expensive style of Flemish bonding, offset by horizontal bands of vitrified purple-black stretchers, the whole effect looking rather out of place in such rural surroundings' (*The Lake Counties, D. Joy*). The building has long been demolished and this section of the branch sadly did not survive into preservation. *Norris Forrest*

52. How railway enthusiasts used to look: plenty of sports jackets in evidence at the Lakeside terminus on 29th May 1960, as ex-LMS 'Mogul' Class 2-6-0 No. 42952 sits at the head of a Stephenson Locomotive Society (SLS) / Manchester Locomotive Society (MLS) 'Northern Fells' rail tour from Manchester. The branch had experienced fluctuating fortunes, all-year passenger workings being withdrawn in 1938 and even the seasonal service being suspended between 1941 and 1946. The end for BR services came in 1965, 'regrettably just after most of the line had been relaid with experimental concrete sleepers'! (*The Lake Counties, D. Joy.*) But the northern section from Haverthwaite to Lakeside returned to its former glory in 1973, as a preserved railway which continues to flourish today, with the signal box once again operational. *Norris Forrest*

53. Arnside station, looking west on 6th June 1968. The station was opened in 1858 by the Ulverston and Lancaster Railway (a company backed by, and later taken over by, the Furness Railway), a year after the opening of the line through to Ulverston over the impressive 50-span viaduct crossing the Kent estuary (beyond the signal box). The platform face in the foreground served the single-track cut-off line to Hincaster Junction on the WCML which carried a Grange-over-Sands to Kendal passenger service from its opening in 1876 until 1942. Its main traffic was coke trains from County Durham to ironworks in Barrow and Millom, allowing them to avoid reversing at Carnforth. The remaining stub of the line closed completely in 1971, and the track was lifted, but Arnside signal box remains in operation today. *Henry Priestley (from Milepost collection)*

54. Ivatt Class 2 2-6-2 tank No. 41217 sits at Coniston's charming terminus station in 1957. Originally conceived as a more efficient way to service local copper mines, the branch from Foxfield on the Cumbrian Coast line opened to passengers in 1859 and increasingly became dependent on tourist traffic. Visitors arrived at a fittingly attractive terminus - albeit high above the village and Coniston Water - with a distinctive 'Swiss cottage' style, overall roof and gabled drystone walls. The Ivatt tanks were light-weight mixed-traffic locos first introduced by the LMS in 1946, but 41217 was built at Crewe Works by BR in 1948. Equipped for 'push-pull' working, it was based at Barrow (11B) from 1950 to 1958 and was latterly employed on station pilot duties at Carlisle Citadel until withdrawal at the end of 1966. *Neville Stead Collection*

55. An Up service on the Cumbrian Coast line (thought to be the late-morning Workington Main to Euston train), comprising a mix of maroon and 'blood and custard' coaches, draws into the junction station at Foxfield in 1957, headed by rebuilt 'Royal Scot' Class 4-6-0 No. 46151 *The Royal Horse Guardsman*. 46151 was based at Crewe North at the time of this photo and enjoyed a peripatetic existence after rebuilding in 1953, finally being withdrawn from Sheffield Darnall in 1962. The Coniston branch can be seen trailing in on the right, with the branch train stabled between duties - the layout here was awkward, with no bay platform and the branch only accessible from the Up platform, hence the need for the branch train to lie-over on a siding north of the station.
Neville Stead Collection

56. Opened in 1848, an enlarged station was built at Foxfield (11½ miles north of Barrow) in 1879: the island platform was widened and a masonry-supported overall roof created above the Down platform. In this 1957 shot looking north an ornate station bench sits beside an LMS 'Hawkseye' running-in board, while a push-pull branch train for Coniston can just be glimpsed at the Up platform. Although the stone structures on the left were subsequently demolished, the timber waiting shelter and attached signal box (out of sight behind the shelter) are still in use, while a steam-era water tower survives on the Up side. The Prince of Wales Hotel (on the far right) was also still in business prior to the Covid pandemic. *Neville Stead Collection*

57. (Opposite) The delightful setting and style of the Coniston terminus is well illustrated here, looking towards Coniston Fells. By the time of this 1960 shot, the line was freight-only, the 1958 closure to passengers being precipitated not just by the general rise in car ownership but also by the specifics of railway geography: the station (located for ease of access to the copper mines) was not convenient for the steamer pier on Coniston Water, and the circuitous route from key visitor markets - via Barrow - contrasted with the more direct access to the likes of Lakeside and Windermere. The station scene is deserted here, and the signal arms have been removed, doubtless reflecting a low-cost 'One Engine in Steam' operation over the 8½ single-track miles from Foxfield. The branch closed completely in 1962. *Neville Stead Collection*

58. In this undated shot, driver and fireman are on the lookout as 'Black 5' No. 45282 pulls a train of 21T hoppers loaded with industrial coal - possibly bound for Millom - through St Bees, while domestic coal waits to be unloaded from 16T mineral wagons on the siding to the left. The extensive West Cumberland coalfield stretched from south of Whitehaven almost to Wigton, between Maryport and Carlisle. The last deep undersea mine closed in 1986, but a new pit is proposed for coking coal at Woodhouse near Whitehaven. 45282 entered service in 1936, and was based at no fewer than 11 sheds post-nationalisation, including Workington from late 1960 until early 1962, suggesting the shot was taken during the spring or summer of 1961. *Neville Stead Collection*

59. An unidentified Metrovick Type 2 on a Carnforth-Workington service approaches the station at Seascale on an unknown date between 1962 and 1968. The 20 'Pilot Scheme' Metrovicks were an early product of BR's 1955 Modernisation Plan, built by Metropolitan-Vickers of Stockton-on-Tees and entering service in 1958-59, initially often used in pairs on the overnight London-Glasgow 'Condor' express freight service (as depicted in Terence Cuneo's *Night Freight* painting). These 1,200hp locomotives were the only two-stroke diesels built under the Pilot Scheme, and had a Co-Bo wheel arrangement (a 6-wheel bogie at one end, a 4-wheel bogie at the other) – unique in British Railways practice. Seascale signal box - to the right of the train - has closed, but leaving a block section of just four miles between Sellafield and Drigg. *Larry Fullwood*

60. Ex-LMS Fowler 4P Class 2-6-4 tank No. 42376 drifts into St Bees station with a northbound train, comprised mainly of non-corridor stock, on the morning of 27th January 1962. Built at Derby Works in 1932, 42376 was based at Barrow from 1951 until its withdrawal in 1962. St Bees station was opened in 1849 and remains open today, with a crossing loop splitting the 11 single-track miles from Sellafield to Whitehaven. The signal box (behind the camera, on the Down side) controlling the loop was built in 1891 in - very unusually for a British box - the 'Arts and Crafts' style, and is now Grade II-listed. Today the Furness Railway timber structure which housed a waiting room on the Down side survives (albeit somewhat modified) as a private dwelling at this now unstaffed station.
Larry Fullwood

61. Metrovick Type 2 No. D5702 hauls the 8.25am Lancaster-Workington past Seascale South signal box and sidings on 18th April 1964. D5702 was the third of the class to enter service - at Derby shed on 29th September 1958 - and was allocated to Barrow in Furness at the time of this photo; it was withdrawn from service on 7th September 1968 after a working life of just 9 years, 11 months and 9 days. The sidings here had formerly served a Royal Ordnance Factory but in 1959 the site became the Drigg 'Low Level Waste Repository', the UK's central long-term store for low-level radioactive waste. It continues to generate rail traffic today, but rail access is now controlled by the signal box at Drigg station, half a mile to the south. *Larry Fullwood*

62. Ex-Furness Railway Pettigrew 0-6-0 No. 52499 - fitted with an L&YR type Belpaire firebox boiler by the LMS at Horwich Works - pulls out of the ex-LNWR part of Whitehaven Bransty station in 1955. The empty coaching stock working is composed of ex-LMS coaches in 'blood and custard' livery which have presumably arrived as a terminating service from Carlisle. There is considerable evidence of recent industrial activity and associated railway infrastructure on both sides in this scene but William Colliery on the left had closed at the end of the previous year and the NCB internal-user wagons visible here would now be redundant. Bransty Junction signal box can be seen to the right of the train while at the far right is the long-closed former LNWR engine shed.
Neville Stead Collection

63. Pettigrew 0-6-0 No. 52494, the only survivor of the class not reboilered in LMS days, eases a long train of empty mineral hoppers towards Bransty Junction where it is signalled through the ex- Furness Railway (FR) platforms at Whitehaven Bransty station and into the single-track tunnel to Corkickle. The shot is undated, but the loco has a Workington shed plate, which it carried for just over a year following its eviction from Moor Row shed on closure of the latter in July 1954. 52494 was eventually withdrawn from service at Barrow in 1956, the year before the last three of the class (including 52499) were withdrawn - the final FR locomotives in service. Coke ovens once located below the cliffs in the background had disappeared prior to 1900 and the landscape already looks very post-industrial. *Neville Stead Collection*

64. 'Black 5' No. 44892 awaits departure from Workington Main at the head of the 1.3pm service to Manchester on 19th August 1959. Entering service in 1945, at the time of this photo 44892 was based at Carnforth shed, where it would remain until its 1967 withdrawal. Workington Station was opened in 1846 by the Whitehaven Junction Railway and was subsequently rebuilt and extended by the LNWR in 1866, incorporating four tracks between the two through platforms. At the height of railway development, two other stations served Workington: Workington Bridge on the Cockermouth and Workington Railway, and Workington Central on the Cleator and Workington Junction Railway, both now closed. Attractive glazed canopies remain in situ at the remaining station today. *W.A.C. Smith*

65. No. D5701 (based at Barrow shed) hauls the 8.25am Carnforth-Workington service along the coast-hugging Whitehaven-Parton section on 8th August 1964. The Metrovicks suffered frequent failures after their 1958-59 introduction to service and by 1961 the entire class had been handed back to the manufacturer for remedial work on the engines and to cure problems with cab windows falling out while running! D5701 spent no fewer than 303 days undergoing heavy repair at Metropolitan-Vickers between October 1961 and August 1962. This loco was one of the last 12 of the class to be withdrawn, on 7th September 1968, all allocated to 'Preston Division' at the time, with D5701 stored in the old steam shed at Kingmoor after withdrawal. One of the Metrovicks - D5705 - has survived into preservation. *Larry Fullwood*

66. Moor Row lay at the heart of the West Cumberland Ore Field, a strip of iron-bearing limestone stretching nine miles north from Egremont, which hand-in-hand with the railway - generated rapid growth in the local iron (and later steel) industry between the 1840s and '80s. A four-road shed, replacing outdated existing facilities, was built by the Furness Railway here in about 1884. In this undated shot, taken prior to closure on 31st July 1954 of the by then two road shed - mining subsidence had necessitated its part-demolition in the 1940s - Pettigrew 0-6-0 No. 52494 simmers between turns at the shed entrance. Built by the North British Locomotive Company in 1913, 52494 was the first of 19 of this largest and most powerful of the mineral engines on the Furness Railway. *Neville Stead Collection*

67. By the time that the SLS / MLS 'West Cumberland Rail Tour' visited Moor Row, hauled by re-boilered 0-6-0 No. 52501, on 5th September 1954, three decades had elapsed (apart from a brief revival in 1946-47) since the station last saw regular public passenger services: north to Siddick Junction; north-east to Frizington, Rowrah and Marron Junction on the Workington-Keswick line; north-west to Mirehouse Junction (Corkickle) and south to Egremont and Sellafield (this through route being the 1946-47 revival). Interestingly, however, both Moor Row and Egremont were in the Beeching Report's list of stations for closure - being served by workmen's trains to Sellafield, which were duly withdrawn in 1965. 52499 – like the rest of the class – was fitted with vacuum brakes and steam heating which permitted it to be used on rail tours. *Neville Stead Collection*

68. Only 11 days before its withdrawal at Workington shed, ex-LMS Class 4F 0-6-0 No. 44192 shunts the 12.57pm Corkickle-Millom freight at Moor Row on 13th April 1965. In this view looking east the line to Egremont and Sellafield diverges to the right beyond the signal box. Ahead, and later curving north, stretches the second route to Cleator Moor, Frizington and Rowrah, opened in 1866 as a diversionary line to avoid mining subsidence on the original route east via Crossfield. By the time of this shot the Siddick Junction line (which diverged near Cleator Moor) had been closed completely south of Distington for two years, while the through freight line beyond Rowrah to Marron Junction had closed in mid-1954 although the track remained in place for a further ten years. But much worse was to come. *Larry Fullwood*

69. One of the last surviving iron ore mines in West Cumberland was at Ullcoats, served by a mile-long branch diverging east from the single-track Moor Row-Sellafield line just south of Egremont. Here ex-Midland Railway Fowler 4F 0-6-0 No. 43964 battles up the branch with the 11am trip from Egremont on 13th April 1965. Entering service in 1921, 43964 had a peripatetic existence during its BR years, shedded variously at Kentish Town, Cricklewood East, Toton, Nottingham and Workington. With ten of the class (three ex-MR and seven ex-LMS) on its books at the start of the year, Workington was amongst the last 4F strongholds but only one example would see out the year, Ivatt class 4 2-6-0s having taken over their duties. *Larry Fullwood*

70 & 71. Having shunted Ullcoats Mine sidings on the late morning of 13th April 1965, 43964 returned tender-first on the 1.55pm trip to Egremont with a trainload of mineral hoppers. In the first shot, looking east, the train is almost running parallel with the line from Beckermet Mines Junction (where a short branch to the ore mine of that name diverged eastwards) and, further south, Sellafield on the Cumbrian Coast route. In the second shot, looking north, the train is heading towards Egremont but still on 'the branch', which joined the Sellafield line just out of sight on the left. At the time of these photos, school and workmen's trains (the latter to and from Sellafield) were still plying the track in the foreground, although the latter would only continue to do so for another five months. The line beyond Beckermet Mines Junction saw its last train in December 1968 when the school trains (an unadvertised passenger service started as late as September 1964, conveying pupils to Wyndham School in Egremont from Seascale in the morning, then home after school) ceased running. The ore mine itself (the last in West Cumberland) and the surviving railway north through Egremont and Moor Row to Corkickle closed in 1980. And so, West Cumberland's rail network now comprises only the Cumbrian Coast line from Barrow to Carlisle – but perhaps we should be thankful for small mercies, as the Beeching Report proposed closure of the entire section from Barrow to Whitehaven. *Larry Fullwood*

Port Carlisle and Silloth

72. Even as long ago as 1953 (with what is thought to be an Austin 18 car evoking the period), trains were a distant memory at the former Port Carlisle station. The 11-mile branch railway from Carlisle opened in 1854 – and for much of its history had a horse-drawn passenger service – but the line (and the port) suffered from competition from the newer, deeper-water port of Silloth to the west. The North British Railway absorbed the local railway (and that to Silloth) in 1880, but despite attempts to reverse the line's declining fortunes with the introduction of a steam railcar in 1928, it closed completely in 1932. Today the remains of the station's single platform can still just be seen and the Hope & Anchor Inn (far right, on Main Street) remains in business.

73. A classic rural railway scene at Kirkandrews in the summer of 1953. The first trains called here in 1854, as part of the Carlisle-Port Carlisle operation, but from 1856 the Carlisle & Silloth Bay Railway & Dock Company's new railway to Silloth provided the train service. A large seed warehouse can be seen by the platform, and another noteworthy sight is the sharp track curvature (with check rail), reflecting the railway's use of the former Carlisle Canal cut, necessitating a permanent speed restriction of 25mph. Evidently, in common with other stations on the line, it had its name picked out in sea shells on a raised area opposite the station building, the latter surviving today - albeit much modified - as a private residence. *Neville Stead Collection*

74. Burgh by Sands was one of the five of the once-nine intermediate stations on the Silloth branch which survived until complete closure in September 1964. The line was among the first in Britain (on 29th November 1954) to see regular timetabled operation by Diesel Multiple Units, significantly cutting operating costs and typically boosting patronage. In the case of the Silloth branch, BR 'Derby Lightweight' DMUs were deployed - the first such trains to be built en-masse for BR (at Derby Works). The last Derby Lightweight units were withdrawn from normal service in 1969, and that year 16 such vehicles (including units which had worked the Silloth branch) were held in store by BR at Carlisle for the putative - and ultimately unsuccessful - Border Union Railway Company bid to re-open the Waverley Route. *W.A.C. Smith*

75. A 'Derby Lightweight' DMU pauses between turns at the Silloth terminus in an undated shot thought to be mid-1964; a trip freight awaits departure in the background. DMUs were not enough to save the line, and it closed on 7th September 1964 'amid scenes of unprecedented hostility. An angry and jeering crowd of an estimated 9,000 people [much larger than the town's population!] packed the terminus and delayed departure of the last train for half an hour, with stones being thrown at the locomotive inspector, detonators placed on the track and dozens of passengers staging a sit-down on the line. Allegedly to prevent any possibility of re-opening, the track was lifted so quickly that several carriages were left stranded at Silloth and had to be dismantled where they stood.' (The Lake Counties, D. Joy.) Neville Stead Collection

76. An unusual visitor to the Waverley Route: York-based B16/3 Class 4-6-0 No. 61439 on a northbound freight battles up the 1 in 100 gradient on the approach to Penton station in an undated shot probably taken during the 1950s. Although unusual, the appearance of one of these with these North Eastern Railway-built mixed-traffic locos (in this case rebuilt by the LNER with Walschaerts valve-gear) was not unique, as at least another five members of the class are known to have worked through Hawick. The Waverley Route is usually associated with Scotland, but the first 21¼ of the 98¼ miles from Carlisle to Edinburgh lay south of the Border, including Penton and five other English stations which closed on 6th January 1969. *Neville Stead Collection*

77. Carlisle Kingmoor-based 'Black 5' No. 44886 has only a brake van in tow as it steams north through Kershope Foot – on one of the few level stretches of the Waverley Route - in an undated shot probably taken before the cessation of regular steam working over the line in January 1966. Kingmoor shed would continue to roster steam in lieu of failed diesels almost up until the depot's closure, the last recorded steam working over the line taking place in November 1967 when 'Britannia' Class No. 70022 Tornado passed through here on the 19.44 Carlisle-Edinburgh passenger service. 44886 will shortly cross into Scotland, the border with England lying along the Kershope Burn just beyond the level crossing. *Norris Forrest*

78. Riddings Junction - seen here looking north, with the Scottish border just a few hundred yards to the left behind the trees - was an interchange station for the Langholm branch, rather than serving any significant local community. There were two facing platforms on the main line, with the Down platform being an island whose outer face was served by branch trains. A small goods yard was located behind the Up platform, accessed by the track just visible to the right of the signal box. The main station building, on the Up platform, was not typical of North British Railway design, and its brick construction may have been due to the presence of a nearby brick works. *Norris Forrest*

Want more...?

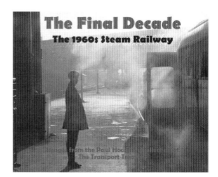

The Final Decade - The 1960s Steam Railway

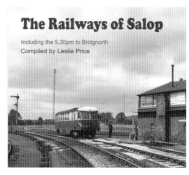

The Railways of Salop - Including the 5:30pm to Bridgnorth

Steam Memories North East Scotland

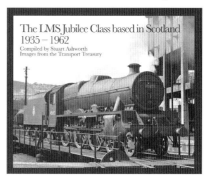

The LMS Jubilee Class based in Scotland 1935 - 1962

Dick Riley: West from Paddington

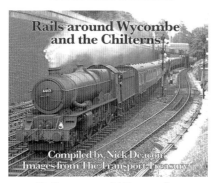

Rails around Wycombe and the Chilterns